GW00644892

THE STORY OF

MVAGUSTA

MOTOR CYCLES

THE STORY OF MV AGUSTA MOTOR CYCLES

Peter Carrick

Foreword by John Surtees

PSL Patrick Stephens, Cambridge

First published in 1979

British Library Cataloguing in Publication Data

Carrick, Peter
  The story of MV Agusta motor cycles.
  1. MV Agusta motorcycle
  I. Title
  796.7'5   TL448.M/

  ISBN 0 85059 303 4

Photoset in 10 on 11 pt English Times by
Manuset Limited, Baldock, Herts. Printed in
Great Britain on 100 gsm Pedigree coated
cartridge and bound by The Garden City Press,
Letchworth, Herts, for the publishers
Patrick Stephens Limited, Bar Hill, Cambridge,
CB3 8EL, England.

Contents

Acknowledgements

I have been helped in the preparation of *The Story of MV Agusta Motor Cycles* by a great many people who have remembered incidents and events, and confirmed reports and conversations. I thank them all and, in particular, express my appreciation to Charlie Rous, Pete Bate, Jeff Clew, Mrs Edna Graham, Stuart Graham, Bill Lomas, Derek Minter and Cecil Sandford.

I am also grateful for the help given by the Auto-Cycle Union, *Motor Cycle News* and *Motor Cycle Weekly*. The extract from *Motor Cycle* is reproduced by permission of IPC Specialist and Professional Press Limited and from *Hailwood* by Mike Hailwood and Ted Macauley by permission of the publishers, Transport Bookman Publications Limited.

The manuscript was typed by Valerie King, Diana Davis, Pat Birchall and Debbie Carrick to whom I also extend my thanks.

Henlow, Beds, 1979   Peter Carrick

Foreword

It gives me particular pleasure to write this foreword to Peter Carrick's book, not simply because I won seven motor cycle World Championships riding MV Agusta motor cycles, but more perhaps because this famous Italian factory made such an outstanding impact, and contributed so much, to motor cycle racing over almost three decades.

Inspired by the drive, energy and single-mindedness of its founder, Count Domenico Agusta, MV occupy a unique position in motor cycle history. Their grand total of 75 individual and manufacturers road racing World Championships and more than 270 grand prix wins is an astonishing record and the factory's dedication to racing, with those memorable four-stroke machines of outstanding quality, attracted all the important racers of the day.

The Story of MV Agusta Motor Cycles is an absorbing and worthy documentation, and a fascinating account, of the most successful racing factory of all. It includes the important races, the significant events and the riders who raced to fame with MV, including Cecil Sandford, Les Graham, Ray Amm, Gary Hocking, Carlo Ubbiali, John Hartle, Mike Hailwood, Phil Read, Giacomo Agostini, of course, and others. The text, which is well illustrated, also gives a fascinating insight into the background and character, not only of Count Domenico Agusta himself, but of the motor cycle factory he founded.

I am sure the book will have enormous appeal, not only to MV Agusta enthusiasts, but to all who follow motor cycle racing.

John Surtees
Edenbridge, Kent.

MV Agusta Story in brief

1946 MV Augusta formed in Italy to make motor cycles. First machine, a 98 cc model, introduced.

1948 Entered racing in the 125 cc class at the Italian Grand Prix with a single-cylinder two-stroke machine.

1949 Development of four-stroke 125 and 500 cc racers.

1950 Ing Remor, designer of the post-war air-cooled Gilera four, joined MV. First grand prix appearance of the four-cylinder 500 cc racer, at the Belgian Grand Prix.

1951 Les Graham, former 500 cc World Champion and AJS team rider, joined MV racing team. First appearance on the Isle of Man with retirements in both the 125 and 500 cc TTs.

1952 First World Championships through Cecil Sandford in the 125 cc individual and manufacturers 125 cc classes. First TT victory through Cecil Sandford in the Lightweight 125 cc race.

1953 Carlo Ubbiali and Luigi Taveri joined the MV racing team. Les Graham won the Lightweight 125 cc TT, but was killed on the second lap of the Senior race. MV retained the 125 cc manufacturers title. Production of the first MV racing 350.

1954 British riders Bill Lomas and Dickie Dale joined the racing team.

1955 Southern Rhodesian Ray Amm signed for MV. Count Agusta decided to contest all four solo classes of the World Championships. Amm was killed in his first race for MV. MV won all six rounds of the 125 cc World Championship and Carlo Ubbiali took the title. MV won 125 and 250 cc manufacturers titles.

1956 John Surtees signed to lead the race team for the next five years. Surtees brought MV their first Senior TT victory. MV won the 125 and 250 cc World Championships through Ubbiali and the 500 cc World Championship through Surtees. Manufacturers titles also secured in the same three classes. Won in all four solo classes at the Belgian Grand Prix. MV Distributors Limited of London formed to import MV Agusta road models.

1957 Mike Hailwood had his first 'unofficial' rides.

1958 Won all four solo World Championships through Ubbiali (125 cc), Provini (250 cc) and Surtees (350 and 500 cc), and all four solo manufacturers titles. John Hartle joined the team.

1959 World titles in all four solo classes through Ubbiali (125 and 250 cc) and Surtees (350 and 500 cc). Manufacturers world titles in all four solo classes.

1960 For the third successive year all four solo classes won through Ubbiali (125 and 250 cc) and Surtees (350 and 500 cc) and all four manufacturers awards. Second in the 125 cc class (Gary Hocking), second (Gary Hocking) and third (Taveri) in the 250 cc class, second (Hocking) in the 350 cc class and second (Venturi) in the 500 cc class. Gary Hocking signed as a replacement for John Surtees, who left to go car racing. Carlo Ubbiali retired.

1961 Withdrawal from 125 and 250 cc racing, but the 350 and 500 cc world titles retained through Gary Hocking; also the manufacturers world titles in the same classes. Mike Hailwood had first 'official' rides for MV at Monza.

1962 Mike Hailwood signed and, through him, MV won the 500 cc world title. Manufacturers title gained in the 500 cc class.

1963 In spite of a challenge from Geoff Duke's Gilera team 500 cc world title again won, through Hailwood. Manufacturers award also gained in in the same class.

1964 Set up new One Hour Record at Daytona, Mike Hailwood the rider. Hailwood again won the 500 cc world crown for MV, who also won the manufacturers title in this class.

1965 The 500 cc individual and manufacturers titles won for the seventh year running. Hailwood was the rider. Introduction of the three-cylinder MV. Italian Giacomo Agostini signed as support rider to Hailwood. First appearance in Britain of the 600 cc four-cylinder roadster.

1966 Hailwood left for Honda and was succeeded as number one rider by Giacomo Agostini. 500 cc world title (Agostini), but lost the manufacturers title in the same class to Honda.

1967 Again won the 500 cc title (Agostini), for the 10th successive time: also regained 500 cc manufacturers award. MV had now won 25 world titles in 15 years and a total of 165 World Championship races, 70 of them in the premier 500 cc class.

1968 First TT Junior and Senior double victory (Agostini) and 500 cc world title. Also recaptured the 350 cc World Championship. Won 350 and 500 cc manufacturers titles.

1969 Agostini's 'double' victories in Spain, West Germany, the Isle of Man, Holland, East Germany, Czechoslovakia, Finland and Northern Ireland to give a 100 per cent record, brought 350 and 500 cc world titles in both the individual and manufacturers categories.

1970 Won all 11 rounds in the 500 cc class and all ten in the 350 cc class to win, through Agostini, the 500 and 350 cc World Championships. Once again manufacturers titles in these classes were secured.

1971 Count Domenico Agusta died in Milan. MV Agusta rider Bergamonti was fatally injured at Riccioni. Through Agostini, again won the 500 and 350 cc world titles and the manufacturers awards.

1972 Agostini took MV to their 15th successive 500 cc world title. Alberto Pagani, signed as a replacement for Bergamonti, took second place. The 350 cc World Championship won (Agostini). Manufacturers awards in both classes. Agostini and MV raced on the Isle of Man for the last time following the fatal crash of Gilberto Parlotti. Phil Read had first rides for MV.

1973 Phil Read signed to the team with Agostini and took the 500 cc world title. Agostini gained the 350 cc world title. The MV three and four gained the 500 cc manufacturers award. The Italian Government secured a 51 per cent interest in MV Agusta.

1974 Agostini left MV Agusta for Yamaha and Read became MV's premier rider. The 500 cc World Championship title won (Read) for the last time, bringing to an end their uninterrupted run of 17 consecutive wins in the class. Lost the 350 cc world title to Yamaha. Gianfranco Bonera signed. Won the 500 cc class at the Belgian Grand Prix for the 17th time in 17 years. Gus Kuhn Motors Limited of London became MV Agusta concessionaires in the UK.

1975 Arturo Magni, MV team manager, celebrated 25 years with the factory.

1976 MV Agusta pull out of racing. Phil Read departed for other rides and Agostini accepted an invitation to ride MV machinery on a private basis.

1977 Gus Kuhn Motors Limited dropped the MV Agusta franchise for the UK. MV announced their retirement from racing. Amalgamation with the already government controlled Ducati concern. Agusta Concessionaires (GB) Limited began importing MV models.

1978 Closure of Agusta Concessionaires (GB) Limited.

1979 Efforts by the Italian Cagiva motor cycles company to acquire the rights to the MV name and the MV racing machinery.

Chapter 1

The move to motor cycles—and Les Graham shows the way

In the early years following the Second World War the tiny village of Verghera, near the small town of Gallarate, hardly warranted a second glance. There was little to distinguish it from the many other similar villages scattered about Northern Italy. A bit run down. Impoverished. Its main feature was to become the Agusta factory which stood, protected by a wood which itself stretched to the perimeter of Malpensa Airport, just a few kilometres from bustling Milan. Here, from a corner of this unprepossessing hamlet, the dogmatic, inflexible Count Domenico Agusta reigned supreme as the head of his firm, Meccanica Verghera.

It was from a corner of his factory complex that the Count built some of the finest, most reliable and most successful racing motor cycles the world has known.

The first MV Agusta race machines did not appear until 1948. They made little impact in a post-war racing world still largely dominated by the British Norton and Velocette factories. Soon, though, multi-cylinder bikes from the Italian Guzzi and Gilera concerns were to eclipse the single-cylinder British machines in the large capacity classes and, while a world title won for him by the Englishman Cecil Sandford as early as 1952 was enough to satisfy Count Agusta for the time being, it was not for another four years that the MV Agusta name began to command real attention. By 1958, following the shock withdrawal from competition of the famous Italian Gilera, Guzzi and Mondial factories, MV were set to take over. In the 20 years from 1958, racing machinery inspired by the Count and built in the Verghera workshop was to take an astronomical 33 individual world titles and 37 manufacturers awards.

Yet, astonishingly, motor cycles were hardly ever more than a hobby for the Count, even though his interest bordered on the obsessional. Compared with the output of, say, Norton in earlier days and certainly the Japanese factories which were still to come, the output of MV's road-going models was always puny, international sales being meagre even in the best years. It was the flag-waving exercise of road racing in grand prix events and in the home-based Italian championships which later excited and consumed the Count most. He seldom went to race meetings, never visited the Isle of Man, yet he charted the progress of his famous scarlet and silver machines on European and world circuits with the attention to detail and the calculating deliberation of a captain easing his ship through a minefield.

The MV company originated in 1923 when Giovanni Agusta, father of Domenico, founded an aircraft factory at Verghera. Within four years the founder was dead, the business passing to his wife, Guiseppina. By this time Domenico was old enough to be involved, but changing times and the defeat of Italy in the war ruined the company, called Construzioni Aeronautiche Giovanni Agusta, and forced the Agusta family to search for business in other directions. Supported by his three younger brothers, Domenico turned to motor cycle manufacture.

That he should do so is not entirely surprising. After all, Italy had a proud legacy, especially of ability in mechanical matters, stretching back almost to the dawn of motorised transport and this must have provided at least a glint of inspiration. Furthermore, there was the glittering example of nearby Gilera, whose successful history of motor cycle racing from the pre-war days of the 1930s had set a precedent. Above all perhaps, it was with the intention of recapturing business prosperity that the proud Agusta family pushed ahead with their plans. For, as former MV works rider Bill Lomas observed: 'Just after the war anything that was moving on two wheels would sell in Europe. There were probably as many as 150 motor cycle makers at that time. There was a motor cycle manufacturer in every village'.

That is when the name of the concern was changed to Meccanica Verghera Agusta, later becoming eminent throughout the world of racing as simply MV, or MV Agusta. In Italy at the time there was a big, existing market for the small-capacity two-stroke and MV Agusta sought to capture some of this profitable business with a 98 cc machine. This first, historic model was a very ordinary machine which followed the normal pattern of the day. It made little impact, but a sports version, introduced in 1946, became popular with competitors in the 125 cc class which was started in Italy at about that time. Reputed to have a top speed of almost 60 mph, it had a three-speed gearbox and telescopic forks.

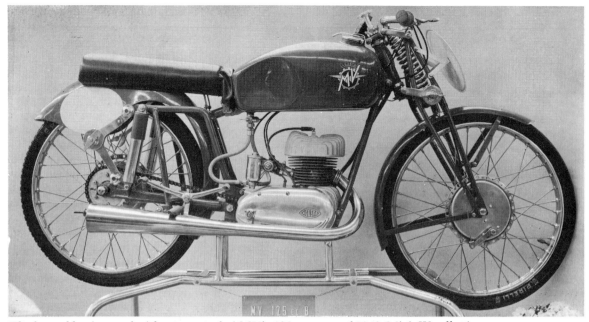

The legend begins, and with a two-stroke! MV's 125 cc racer of 1949 (Mick Woollett).

It was customary in those early post-war years to follow the pre-war example of gaining commercial recognition through racing successes; it followed that Count Agusta should push ahead strongly with plans for a specially designed racer. With motor cycling so closely allied to sport, racing was recognised, in Britain at any rate, as being important in efforts to lift morale following the devastation of war. Perhaps it was the same in Italy. Further incentive came from the international body of motor cycling which, while denying Germany official entry in international competition because of her war history, nevertheless allowed the Italians to enter. A re-structuring of international road racing through the formation of the modern World Championships in 1949 was yet another important factor in the revival of the sport.

To gain publicity for his product Count Agusta unveiled his first real racer in 1948, a single-cylinder two-stroke with a four-speed gearbox. It was this machine which brought him his first significant success, Italian rider Bertoni causing great excitement at the MV factory by winning the 125 cc class of the Italian Grand Prix that year. It was, however, an isolated success, for Mondial, also from Italy, through the skill and vision of their designer Alfonso Drusiani, were producing superbly built double overhead camshaft machines which overwhelmed all opposition and, although of only 125 cc capacity, were faster than many of the then current 250 and 350 cc bikes.

A class of racing which until then had been

regarded as being of little importance, instantly rose in stature because of these excellent machines which were totally to dominate the 125 cc class of the new World Championships in 1949. The MV two-stroke was outclassed, though in Switzerland Cavaccuiti came third and Bertoni sixth, while in Holland Clemencigh rode second to Nello Pagani on the superior Mondial.

Mondial's dominance forced MV back into the development shop and for a year they concentrated on catching up with the opposition. By early 1950 they were ready with a double overhead camshaft 125 cc racer the engine of which bore a striking resemblance to the 250 cc Benelli. Sadly the new machines were again out-paced in a class which once more reeled to the onslaught of the mighty little Mondials. At Assen, in the opening round, Mondial machines claimed four of the five top places, Benasedo on the MV finishing in sixth position. In Belfast, there were only two finishers— both on Mondial machines—out of seven starters, and at Monza, in the final grand prix, Mondials finished in the top six places.

None the less, 1950 was to be a significant year for MV. The shrewd Count Agusta, his ambitious eye already sharply focused on the heavier, more fashionable machine classes, had during the previous winter approached Ing Pietro Remor, the mechanical wizard who had designed the remarkable post-war, air-cooled Gilera four, and persuaded him to leave the neighbouring Arcore factory of Gilera, where he was a consultant, for a new berth with MV. Remor joined Gilera's former chief mechanic, Arturo Magni. At the time Magni was only a junior mechanic, but it was he who worked so well with Les Graham in later years to develop the heavier MVs and he was to remain with the company right through their most glorious racing years until the factory disappeared as a force in World Championship competition. Together, Remor and Magni headed a development team which designed and built the first MV four within just six months.

Having by now become fully committed to the four-stroke principle, MV resisted all temptations to move over to two-stroke machines and in the late 1960s and early '70s were to defend, almost single-handed, the two-stroke attack from Japan. This first and historic MV 500—for it was in the highly prestigious 500 cc class that MV were to secure their most outstanding successes—had its first outing at the Belgian Grand Prix of 1950. Behind two Gileras, an AJS and another Gilera, Italian rider Arciso Artesiani finished fifth. Before a home crowd at Monza in the final round of the series the MV did even better, finishing in third position behind a Norton ridden by Geoffrey Duke (who that year was to go on to win his first world title) and the Gilera of Umberto Masetti.

Not surprisingly, this first MV 500 resembled the Gilera, but Remor brought in a number of new ideas. The basic form was of an in-line four with a four-speed gearbox and, unlike the Gilera, it had shaft final drive. It had unusual blade-type girder forks and the 'parallel ruler' type of swinging arm, both forms of suspension dependent on torsion bars. Bore and stroke were 52 mm × 58 mm and a power output of 52 bhp at 9,500 rpm was claimed. A unique feature was the gear change arrangement. There was a pedal on each side. The rider pushed down with his heel on the left pedal for upward changes and on the right to change down. The machine had four straight-through exhaust pipes when first ridden, but the system was fitted with megaphones when Artesiani, appropriately enough himself a former Gilera rider, gave it its first serious

MV's four-cylinder racing design of 1950 (Mick Woollett).

MV Agusta, a new name in racing, at the Italian Grand Prix of 1950. Reg Armstrong is the rider (Mick Woollett).

outing in the Belgian Grand Prix of 1950. Brief specifications of the machine are as follows:

Engine	Four-in-line mounted transversely 500 cc dohc; drive to camshafts by gear train between inboard cylinders; two carburettors with 'V' inlet manifolds.
Ignition	Magneto.
Transmission	Five-speed gearbox in unit with engine final drive by shaft and bevels.
Frame	Duplex cradle with single top-tube and box section rear members; rear springing of parallel ruler type with two swinging arms, controlled by torsion bars.
Forks	Girder pattern controlled by torsion bars.

Tests had shown it to have outstanding potential, though its handling characteristics were to temper optimism with a degree of caution. Three of the new machines were scheduled for their debut in the Isle of Man that year, to be ridden by the Italian trio of

Artesiani, Bertoni and Magi, but the machines were not ready in time. Artesiani's fifth place in Belgium suggests a mediocre performance, but this was not the case. Reaching a race average of 99.83 mph round the sweeping Spa circuit, the MV was less than a minute slower than the winning Gilera of Umberto Masetti. The race is remembered also for the crash involving Les Graham, then 500 cc World Champion, and Norton rider Artie Bell. The latter was so severely injured that he had to end his racing career.

The MV machine was a particularly clean design but, although it showed potential in 1950, its handling left much to be desired and the machine was to see many modifications before MV became a major force in 500 cc racing. Remor found little consolation in the 125 cc class, for although he had also produced a new single-cylinder, 125 cc, overhead cam machine and two of them had been raced in Holland without success, Benasedo's fifth place in the same race (the best that MV could do) had been achieved on one of the earlier two-stroke racers.

MV Agusta, none the less, were on their way.

If Domenico Agusta's recruitment of Gilera's ace boffins Ing Remor and Arturo Magni was the first major step forward for MV, then the signing of British rider Les Graham was surely the next. Italy was not short of good riders, but most were not really world class. The exceptions were spoken for in 1950. Bruno Ruffo and one of the best lightweight riders of all time, Carlo Ubbiali—then at the start of a road racing career which was to bring him seven World Championships and 31 classic wins in the next ten years—were with Mondial. Ruffo also rode Guzzi machinery. Runner up in the 1949 250 cc World Championship, Dario Ambrosini, was busy riding for Benelli, while in the 500 cc class Umberto Masetti and Nello Pagani were with the Gilera team.

However, although Gilera, through the efforts of Masetti, took the 500 cc world title that year, one point ahead of Geoffrey Duke on the Norton, Britain and British riders were still strong runners in a class in which Count Agusta was determined to find a place for MV. He decided his best chance of success would be to recruit a British rider. Duke must have been a strong candidate, particularly at the end of 1950, for in his first season as a works rider, with Norton, he had made astonishing impact, scoring a remarkable 350/500 cc double at Monza to add to wins in the Senior TT and the 500 cc Ulster Grand Prix. Artie Bell, but for his crash in Holland, Bob Foster, Bill Lomas, Reg Armstrong, Dickie Dale and Cecil Sandford all might well have caught Domenico Agusta's eye but, in the end, after the Italian Grand Prix at Monza at the end of 1950 when he finished second to Geoffrey Duke, AJS team leader Les Graham was the man the Count approached with a contract.

Les was an excellent and, in some ways, an obvious choice. He had more development experience than many of the other riders and, in addition, was a formidable opponent on the circuit, proving his abilities by winning the 500 cc World Championship in 1949. MV's need at that time was not only a rider of world class, but a clever mechanic who could also help sort out their machines from the practical standpoint of racing experience.

Graham had made a big name in Britain in the immediate pre-war years racing round the tight Cadwell Park circuit. After war service as a bomber pilot with the RAF, for which he gained the DFC, he resumed his racing career by joining the AJS works team. On the temperamental 'Porcupine' AJS, he went into the record books by becoming the first ever 500 cc World Champion in 1949 after international racing had been reorganised. He won two out of the six grand prix races and would have realised his dearest ambition by winning the Senior TT, but a failed magneto put him out of the running when he had a very secure lead and he was forced to push his bike home.

Les Graham was a dedicated racer and a devoted motor cycle man. British factories had seen their best days and, as a professional racer, he was becoming frustrated by the outlook and attitude of the AJS concern. On the other hand Italy seemed to be alive with motor cycle activity and he was impressed with the developments going on there. He joined MV with relish and set to work immediately. Within a very short time he transformed the 500 cc machine. It took on a more conventional appearance with telescopic front forks and a rear swinging arm controlled by hydraulically damped suspension units replacing the torsion bar controlled blades of the original design. The shaft drive was retained, however, but the unusual gearchange arrangement was replaced by an orthodox system.

It was typical of the Italian approach at the time that riders were often general all-rounders. They

First appearance of the 500 cc MV, at the Belgian Grand Prix of 1951. Arturo Magni, later team manager, is the young mechanic on the left (Mick Woollett).

The 125 cc machine which appeared at the Italian Grand Prix in 1951. Matucci finished sixth (Mick Woollett).

would be race shop mechanics and would also, in addition to racing, be expected to be test riders and to carry out a certain amount of development work. While this approach was probably good enough for the Italian races, something more was required to make an impact on the World Championships. For 1951 Les Graham led a team composed, initially, of three riders—former Gilera rider Bandirola, Artesiani and himself—with Bertacchini joining the team later in the season. In the opening round of the 500 cc championship in Spain, Artesiani and Bandirola stirred emotions in the MV camp and raised hopes with a third and a fifth place, but MV's challenge was to diminish against the might of Gilera and a remarkable performance by Geoffrey Duke on a Norton. At this stage there was no doubt that the Gileras were faster than the MVs and, as yet, the acceleration and outright speed of even the best fours were not enough to compensate fully for the infinitely superior handling of the singles— hence Duke's successful performances on the Norton. On the Isle of Man that year, Graham

retired in both the 125 and 500 cc races on the MVs. By this time the 500 had exchanged the girder forks for telescopics.

It turned out to be a bad year for MV and, even with a new version of their 125 cc machine, there was little success. The best performance came from Les Graham, finishing third behind Italian riders Leoni on a Mondial and Zinzani on a Morini in the Dutch Grand Prix. Too often the MVs suffered mechanical problems.

A good deal of re-thinking was necessary and Graham set to work once more. He toiled tirelessly. Given a free hand on development by Count Agusta, he needed to stabilise the chassis and sort out the mechanical problems. New engines and new frames were built for 1952, Les bringing in an old associate from the Velocette days, Ernie Earles, to assist with the forks and frame. Power was increased to 55 bhp at 10,000 rpm. The engine had a bore and stroke of 53 mm × 56 mm with a carburettor for each of the four cylinders (though only two were later used for racing) and the new machines had five-speed gearboxes with chain drive to the

Above *MV's first appearance on the Isle of Man in 1951. Les Graham, seen on the four-cylinder 500 cc machine, retired in both the Senior and Lightweight 125 cc TTs* (Mick Woollett). **Below** *A close-up of the MV with modified Earles forks* (Mick Woollett).

Above *Graham puts the 500 through its first tests with the Earles forks at Monza in 1952* (Mick Woollett). **Below** *The 500 cc MV which was ridden into third place by the Italian rider Carlo Bandirola at the Swiss Grand Prix of 1952* (Mick Woollett).

rear wheel. Mid-season saw the MV with conventional rear springing and an Earles front fork; the sides of the tank had been shaped to conform to the rider's arms and knees. Two exhaust pipes on each side were merged into a single megaphone.

The prospects looked much better as Bandirola finished third in the opening 500 cc grand prix at Berne in Switzerland, to be followed by a brilliant fighting ride on the Isle of Man by Les Graham as he tussled with Reg Armstrong on a Norton. After riding second to Duke's Norton for four laps, Graham was eventually forced to surrender his place to Armstrong as an oil leak earlier in the race had slowed him down and a missed gear caused a loss of 800 rpm, resulting in a long pit stop: but even then MV might have won had the race been a fraction longer, for the Norton's primary chain broke as Armstrong crossed the line to win. Nonetheless, it was a good week for MV on the island. Cecil Sandford had been given an MV for the Isle of Man and, at a race average of 75.54 mph, won the Lightweight 125 cc TT, also setting the fastest lap at 76.07 mph. The victory was significant, for not only was it MV's first victory on the historic island, but the prelude to their first world title, won by Sandford that very year. More of that later.

Ill-luck in the 500 cc championship was to rob the team of a possible double world title. With no points from the Dutch and Belgian rounds they battled gamely in Germany on the Solitude circuit, Graham finishing in fourth position. Masetti, on the Gilera, who had won in both Holland and Belgium, was leading the championship table, but if Les's luck had been better in the Ulster Grand Prix, he might have ended up with the title, though no-one knew that at the time. The MV led the race for six laps and Les produced a magnificent record lap at 105.94 mph, before being forced to retire, with the rear tyre having been stripped bare of tread after it fouled the mudguard on the bumpy Clady course. It was left to former AJS rider, Bill Lomas, who had been recruited to the MV team, to produce the best MV result in Ireland, finishing third behind the Gilera of McCandless and the AJS of Coleman.

In outstanding style, Les Graham took the 500 cc MV to victory in the two remaining rounds at Monza and Barcelona. In the Italian Grand Prix he led the race from beginning to end and set up the fastest lap, as well as finishing third in the 125 cc race. In the Spanish Grand Prix the MV was again first home in the 500 cc event, with Les riding the 125 cc machine into second place. At Monza the Italian crowd went wild and gave Graham an overwhelming ovation.

This grandstand finish took Graham and the MV to second place in the 500 cc class and to within just three points of the eventual 500 cc World Champion for 1952, Umberto Masetti, on the Gilera. If Count Agusta was disappointed at getting thus far, but not far enough, he could gain considerable consolation from Cecil Sandford's remarkable performance in bringing MV their first ever World Championship that year.

Les Graham's decision to leave AJS and accept the MV offer was beginning to prove successful—for himself and for his team. The British factories were complacent, living off past glories. The money being offered to works riders was meagre and even the country's top riders were expected to work more for the honour and glory than the money. The once incomparable Norton had been eclipsed by Gilera and even the patriotic Geoffrey Duke had found that the only possible way he could ride his way to a world title was to leave the British factory and 'go foreign', signing a Gilera contract.

Les Graham had been spending most of his time in Italy at the MV works and riding in the Continental grands prix, so for the 1953 season he decided to leave England and set up home with his wife and two sons in Italy. Count Agusta had an attractive home up in the mountains not far from Verghera which he used as a holiday home and, by this time, Les had become enough of a colleague and a friend of the MV boss to be allowed to take over the place and move in with his own family. The Agustas' family home was Casina Costa, a luxury villa adjacent to the MV works.

The future looked bright and obviously the combination of MV Agusta and Les Graham had much to offer. Les was beginning to make for himself a fine career in Italy, for by this time MV were also about to advance plans for links with the Bell helicopter company in the United States and, when Les won at Monza in 1952, Larry Bell of the American company was there. According to Bill Lomas, Les did some of the early liaison work and was being groomed as the manager of the Count's new business venture once his racing days were at an end.

Sadly, that end was to arrive all too swiftly but, at the beginning, 1953 had all the signs of being successful for MV. Cecil Sandford, now proudly an MV World Champion, would be riding in 500 cc races as well as on the 125 cc bike and Carlo Ubbiali had been signed to an MV contract, a most significant move, as his succession of wins on MV machines over the following years was to prove. The team were optimistic as Les Graham, on his favoured Isle of Man course, scored a record-breaking victory for MV in the Lightweight 125 cc race and looked a strong contender for the Senior race the next day. But on the second lap of the Senior, while lying second, Les raced the MV into the dip at Bray Hill, lost control, crashed and was killed instantly.

Graham's loss so devastated Count Agusta and the entire Agusta family that the MV team was withdrawn from the 500 cc classics and did not reappear until Monza, later in the season.

Count Agusta's characteristically bold move in signing Les Graham from AJS had worked well. A cheerful, friendly, popular personality with a lot of dash and talent on a motor bike, Les had worked himself almost into the ground to bring the MVs up to world standard. His path had not been easy, for the Count could be difficult to work with and in the beginning the language problem was a further handicap. Yet in a short time Les Graham's dedication, singlemindedness and spontaneous sense of humour struck a chord with the Italian, who admired his talent and his knowledge. Even at that time Count Agusta ruled MV with a rod of iron and if he was away no-one dared make a decision. Les eventually got that changed. Both Cecil Sandford and Bill Lomas remarked on the respectful relationship which existed between the Count and Les. Said Bill: 'Les *was* MV racing'.

Stuart Graham, racing son of Les, commented recently: 'I was only young at the time, but I think that dad was closer to the Agusta brothers than any rider before or since. When we lived in Italy we were very much part of the Agusta family. At the time, MV needed him just as much as he needed them. Later they had become used to their success and were more autocratic'.

The other point which, after his death, added to MV's total respect for Les Graham was that he never left the factory for another contract. Stuart said: 'He was taken from them and it took Domenico a long time to get over the tragedy'.

MV continued to compete in the 125 cc class after Graham's death. Carlo Ubbiali, who had earlier ridden MV machines in International Six Days Trial events, and Cecil Sandford went after MV's second world title. Mondial were having to re-think the design of their now outdated machines and offered little threat to MV, but into their place stepped the German NSU company whose factory racers, ridden principally by Werner Haas, proved virtually unbeatable. The handsome Bavarian won three of the six 125 cc grands prix that season and, although MV won the same number, their success came from three different riders—Les Graham on the Isle of Man, Ubbiali in Germany and Copeta in Spain. NSU took the title by ten points, but MV riders occupied the following four places through Sandford (second), Ubbiali, Copeta and Graham. In the 500 cc class, MV came into the picture again in Italy with Cecil Sandford and the German rider, H.P. Muller, finishing fifth and sixth. Bandirola did even better in the final round of the season in Spain by finishing second behind the Guzzi of Fergus Anderson.

The year that had started bright and hopefully for MV had run headlong into tragedy. Hopes of repeating their success in the 125 cc class had not materialised and the promise of a 500 cc title, which Graham had given them on what was to be his final visit to the Isle of Man, had also been dashed. Most of all they had lost not only their racing team leader but also a man who had been responsible for so much of the development work on the four-cylinder racers.

Individual titles had eluded MV in 1953, but the 125 cc manufacturers world title which they had won in 1952 was retained for 1953 and the year was also notable, in view of MV's much later success in the class, for the production of their first racing 350, which was a scaled-down version of the 500 cc bike. It had a bore and stroke of 47.5 mm × 49 mm and produced around 40 bhp at 10,500 rpm. At this early stage of development, however, the 350 MV was not a success. Les Graham rode it in the Junior TT that year but was forced to retire in the early stages when the engine seized.

It was to be another four years before the 500 MV began to gain the ascendancy in grand prix racing, but it would be unjust to rush ahead without dwelling for a moment on that not inconsiderable achievement by Cecil Sandford in 1952 which brought MV their first ever world title.

Chapter 2

1952—and the first world title

Cecil Sandford performed the deed. Les Graham master-minded it. The result was the first ever TT win and the first ever World Championship for MV—a trifle surprising, perhaps, but the fore-runner to a vast catalogue of title successes to be won by the Italian factory in the following 25 years.

Cecil, by his own admission, was not the greatest odds-on favourite of all time to win the 125 cc TT that year. Carlo Ubbiali on the lightweight Mondial was a much more exciting prospect, but on the day there was no-one better than Sandford and he had an uneventful ride to victory to give MV maximum points in the opening round of the championship series.

He had graduated to road racing in 1949 after two years of grass track racing and scrambling. His debut on the Isle of Man was in 1950 when, riding a Velocette, he finished 33rd in the Junior event and retired in the Senior race. A year later the perform-ance was hardly more impressive, as he retired in the Senior TT. Though respected in Britain as a talented rider, particularly on lighter machinery, Sandford's best years were yet to come. In three previous years of World Championship racing he had made little international impact: fifth in the 350 cc Ulster and sixth in the 350 cc Italian Grands Prix on an AJS in 1950; fifth in the 250 cc and a most creditable second in the 350 cc race of the Swiss Grand Prix of 1951, both on Velocettes; and, that same year, a fourth (Velocette again) in the 350 cc race of the Belgian Grand Prix.

Sandford's opportunity to ride MV in the 1952 TT came about in quite casual fashion. Les Graham was by this time, of course, contracted to MV, but as a professional racer he was interested in compet-ing in more events than could be provided by the Italian factory's works rides, especially on the Isle of Man, which continued to mean so much to British riders and manufacturers. Les had maintained contact with Velocette, for whom both he and Cecil had ridden with distinction in earlier years and, indeed, he rode with consistency a privately-owned 350 cc Velocette KTT in the early part of the previous season.

It was clear that the old, pre-war, single-cylinder designs, with which the British factories had once led the world, were now virtually at the end of their development. The multi-cylinder engines, of mainly Italian design, were set to take over in racing and by 1952 there was a general air of depression in the British motor cycle industry. Velocette were to capitulate completely at the end of that year, closing down their racing department and putting their machines and spares up for sale. In a final fling on the island they gave a works 348 cc KTT ride to Cecil Sandford, who also had a BSA entry in the Senior, and a 250 cc works KTT to Les Graham. Les also intended competing in the Junior race on the private Velocette which had, in the previous season, given him a World Championship win in Switzerland and a second place in Spain.

Graham, faced with the possibility of four rides in the TT, arrived unexpectedly one day at the Sandford home in Shipston, Warwickshire. He

Cecil Sandford, the British rider who brought MV their first world title, in 1952 (Mick Woollett).

19

Sandford in action on the 125 cc MV during his World Championship year. He previously rode for Velocette and Moto Guzzi (Mick Woollett).

offered Cecil a ride. Being slimmer than Graham, Sandford was more suited to the lighter machinery, so the two agreed that it would be better for Sandford to take the 125 cc MV, leaving Graham to concentrate on the bigger machine in the Senior and the works and private Velocettes in the Lightweight 250 cc and Junior 350 cc TTs. This gave them three rides each.

There was no contract, nothing written down. Said Cecil recently: 'Les came and asked me if I was interested in the MV ride. I said I was and that was it'. Nor was the race itself in any way spectacular. 'I was not challenged. It was simply a matter of keeping it going at the right speed', remembered Sandford. Before the race he and Graham had discussed tactics and had gone round the course together. Sandford said: 'A lot of thought went into it. It was windy, as I recall, and Les and I decided which side of the road to ride on at various parts of the course to gain the most benefit from the wind:

like deciding to keep close to a hedge or a wall if the wind was blowing from that direction'.

Before his TT win Cecil Sandford had not even been over to Italy to see the MV factory. It was all such a casual arrangement that even afterwards he was not given a proper written contract. 'I just went along with Les', said Cecil. 'He told me what to do and in turn told the MV people what he was doing. Les had a remarkably free hand on the racing side of MV and what he said was law.'

After the TT victory Graham returned to Italy taking Sandford with him to square things with Count Agusta; then it was on to the Dutch TT, where Sandford made another remarkable impact. He not only outstripped Ubbiali's strong challenge on the Mondial once again, but also defeated three other Italian riders—one on a Morini and two on MV bikes. Not quite the same success was achieved in Germany. Werner Haas, leading the NSU challenge, took the race from Ubbiali, with

Sandford down in third place. Even so, the MV rider was still strongly placed for the title. With two wins out of three races, Sandford led the championship table at this point and went further ahead when he won in Ireland. The Ulster Grand Prix that year produced only eight starters in the 125 cc event and three machines finished the course—all MVs. Morini, through Mendogni, proved superior in Italy, with Graham the best MV rider in the 125 cc class in third place, but Sandford's third position in the final grand prix of the season in Spain was sufficient to give him and MV the world title. He finished four points ahead of Ubbiali, his nearest challenger, and MV also took the 125 cc manufacturers award for the year.

With the British factories' racing effort sadly crumbling, there were a lot of riders looking elsewhere for contracts and, when MV produced the necessary document and asked Cecil Sandford to sign, he did not hesitate. The contract was for two seasons, 1953 and '54, and Cecil said recently that it was a good deal for those days. 'You were paid so much and everything you won you kept— and all expenses were paid', he said.

As already noted, the season began magnificently for MV with Les Graham winning the 125 cc TT on the Isle of Man, Cecil Sandford finishing in third place. MV Agusta machines occupied five of the top six positions. Then came Graham's fatal accident and Sandford, along with other members of the team and all the gear, were shipped back to Italy. Domenico insisted that every effort be made to find the cause of Graham's accident and at Monza dozens of different types of frames were tested. Said Cecil: 'We went round and round Monza with all sorts of 500s trying to find out what might have gone wrong. We nearly made a groove, we went round so many times. But Monza is not the Isle of Man and we weren't able to find out anything which gave a pointer to the cause of the accident. There was a feeling that it was something to do with the front forks, but we discovered nothing'.

For 1953 Count Agusta had signed up Carlo Ubbiali and the talented Italian combined with Cecil Sandford to lead the 125 cc challenge into the new season. They finished second and third in Holland, a reasonable result which was followed by a good win for Ubbiali in Germany. Sandford ran second in the Ulster Grand Prix and second again in the final round in Spain, with Ubbiali collecting a third place at Monza. Werner Haas on the NSU took the title, with Sandford in second place, ten points in arrears, and Ubbiali two further points behind in third position.

Cecil Sandford rode many fine races during his career, but for the man who brought MV Agusta their first world title, the race that started it all off— the Lightweight 125 cc TT on the Isle of Man in 1952—is, perhaps not altogether surprisingly, the race he remembers best of all.

21

Chapter 3

Bidding for racing's top honours

In 1954 and '55 MV Agusta racing was gathering momentum. Les Graham's loss was still acutely felt in the race department and, while further development work took place during the winter, the machines were substantially the same when they were brought out for the grands prix at the start of 1954. Top MV runner with the 125 cc machine was now Carlo Ubbiali, a magnificently successful rider of the future and, although Cecil Sandford's peak days with the Italian factory were over, he too was MV-mounted during 1954. The close season had witnessed the departure from MV of Ing Remor, but Magni remained and Count Agusta's enthusiasm did not waver. On the Isle of Man that year Ubbiali and Sandford kept MV in the picture with a second and third place respectively in the Lightweight 125 cc TT. There was little else in this class for MV to get excited about until Monza, where four Italian riders on MVs were among the first five home—Provini on a Mondial finishing between Sala, the winner, with Ubbiali in third place. The German rider Scheidhuer made it a field day for MV among the results with a sixth position. Ubbiali ended the year second to Rolf Hollaus (NSU) in the 125 cc World Championship.

MV by now were showing interest in the 350 cc class, as well as maintaining their activity with 125 cc and 500 cc racers, but it was a blow to their hopes with the heavier machinery when the fearless Bandirola crashed at the start of the season and broke both arms. Count Agusta, meantime, recruited British riders Dickie Dale and Bill Lomas to strengthen the team, but generally the season was to be disappointing. Beaten by NSU in 125 cc racing, they had no answer to the power of Guzzi in the 350s and the only grand prix win recorded in the 500 cc class was the last meeting in Spain, when Dickie Dale came home ahead of Kavanagh on the Guzzi.

Bill Lomas, a rider of outstanding merit but with a forthright and outspoken personality, had been tempted away from NSU by a more handsome three-year contract with MV. He and Les Graham had been good friends (Cecil Sandford making up a well-known threesome) and his first contacts with Count Agusta had been through Les himself, when Bill was also living on the Continent and riding for NSU. For a while the two riders had stayed at the Ambassador Hotel in Milan. Lomas had begun to make a name for himself back in 1950 when he joined Bob Foster in the Velocette works team, after which there came a spell with AJS before he signed for NSU.

His first rides for MV had been in 1952 when he raced the 125 into second place in the Ulster, but at Monza the motor broke down and in Spain the throttle cable snapped. Graham had looked to Lomas as an MV partner for 1953, but nothing came of it, so Bill was, in some respects, not an altogether surprising candidate for a place with MV once Les had gone. Disappointingly, Bill's time with MV turned out to be short and not very successful. Within a year he had broken off his contract, complaining that Count Agusta would not listen to his ideas to improve the machines. 'The Count could be pig-headed at times', commented Bill recently. 'I could never get along with the Earles forks, but he insisted on keeping them because Les had won at Monza with them. He did change them eventually. The organisation could be pretty chaotic. I remember on the Isle of Man in 1954 they arrived very late with three different kinds of frame and expected them all to be fully tested in a couple of days or so.' Bill emphasised that his split with MV was amicable and, in any event, he came back strongly into the MV story the very next year when he was invited to ride a new 205 cc machine at the TT.

For MV, however, 1954 was a particularly lean year. They had no answer to the all-conquering NSUs in the 125 cc class and against the heavier Guzzi machines could make no headway. Both NSU and Guzzi had long and glorious histories to support them. Guzzi had moved into racing in the early 1920s and consistently favoured the unusual horizontal single-cylinder engine. The great Stanley Woods brought them TT victories in the mid-1930s and, still using the horizontal single-cylinder engine, Guzzi dominated the 250 cc class after the war. They astonished the racing world by moving into the 350 cc class in 1953 and winning the World Championship that same year through the British rider Fergus Anderson.

NSU were racing their machines even earlier, appearing regularly at the TTs from the early 1900s until the outbreak of the First World War. Again in the 1930s, the German factory consistently supported racing. In the late 1930s they developed supercharged twin-cylinder 350 and 500 cc machines and, after Germany had been re-admitted to the FIM in 1950 and following the banning of superchargers, introduced a 500 cc four-cylinder machine with atmospheric induction. They were also busy in speed records and it was on a streamlined supercharged 500 cc twin that Wilhelm Herz became the first man to reach 180 mph on a motor cycle.

Against these illustrious pedigrees, MV could do little in 1954, and at the end of the year Count Agusta had convinced himself that he needed a new rider of stature to take over as MV torch-bearer from the late Les Graham. He found him in the talented Southern Rhodesian, Ray Amm. Ray had come to Britain in 1951 to make his fame and fortune on the race track. Riding his own two Nortons he quickly attracted the attention of Norton chief Joe Craig, who offered him a works contract. A year later he had become Norton team leader and on the Isle of Man in 1953 he won both the Junior and Senior TTs, only the fifth rider to that date to accomplish the double in the same year.

Intensely patriotic, Ray Amm had chosen to stick with British machinery in 1954, in spite of a number of tempting offers, and against exceptional odds he managed to win the Senior TT for Norton in that year and finished runner-up in both the 350 and 500 cc World Championships. Respected and religious, he was a fearless, daring rider with a quiet obsession to win, a trait which produced a succession of hair-raising rides. In 1955 Norton decided they could no longer fully contest the World Championships and Ray Amm had no real alternative but to further his career with a non-British factory. MV saw their chance, stepped in and offered him a good contract. His know-how gained with the British factory was a useful bonus for the Italian team.

Count Agusta responded to the disappointments of 1954 with characteristic gestures. He decided to contest all four solo classes and got the race department fully stretched producing an enlarged version of the 125 for the 250 cc class. Work on the 350 four was held up as the new, lighter machine was given top priority. Models emerged which, at around 200 lb, weighed little more than the 125 bikes and with a bore and stroke of 63 mm × 69 mm and a capacity of 204 cc, were expected to give the MV a good chance of the title, particularly since the remarkably fast twin-cylinder 'Rennmax' works NSUs would be absent in the new season following the German factory's decision to withdraw from

Southern Rhodesian Ray Amm, who took over MV's racing challenge after Les Graham's death. Ray, too, died racing. He is seen here on the Isle of Man in 1952 with his Norton Senior TT machine before he signed for MV (Mick Woollett).

racing.

Ubbiali was MV's top lightweight rider now and while Cecil Sandford's contract did not officially expire until the end of the year, mutual interest was waning as he looked increasingly towards DKW and Guzzi for his future rides. Count Agusta completed his team by signing Remo Venturi and Luigi Taveri.

After bringing MV their first World Championship, Sandford's decline as a works rider for the Italian factory was saddening. His reputation with MV never again reached the 1952 peak and after Graham's death he gradually found the situation less and less to his liking. From then on he was backwards and forwards to Italy and he met Domenico, his mother and brothers. Cecil recalls: 'In the beginning the factory was poor and small. The whole thing was in its infancy and it looked little better than a kind of army dump. The race shop was a bit better. When I first went there, there seemed to be little going on and they didn't appear to be producing many bicycles, but of course it got better and quickly snowballed. During my time they were beginning to think seriously about the helicopter business and once when I was there they had an American showing them how the work should be done'.

Sandford remembers that Count Agusta was always very busy and difficult to approach. He said that Les Graham was the only man who could walk into his office without knocking and there was no doubt that they got on well together. 'Les brought out Agusta to the full. Domenico ran the lot and had more than a casual say in the design of the engine used in the 125 cc MV which won the TT', said Sandford. After Graham's death, Cecil had to deal with Count Agusta himself. 'He used to get a bit mad sometimes and then there would be a lot of shouting going on. But he was a clever man and he lived for the business', said Sandford. He was, 'typically Italian, but a very nice and generous man'.

By this time the Italian riders were coming on well and, according to Sandford, once Les had gone the best bikes began to go to them and the British riders were not very happy with the machines. Ubbiali was showing excellent form and Cecil began strengthening his links with DKW and Guzzi. He said: 'MV could be a bit brutal. If they found a better man then you were out'.

However, while Cecil Sandford was beginning to drift away, Ray Amm was set to spearhead the MV challenge in the heavier classes, but tragedy struck once more when, in his very first race for his new factory, in the 350 cc class at the non-championship Imola meeting in Italy, he crashed and was killed instantly when he struck a post. It was a crushing

Carlo Bandirola in grand prix action on the MV in 1953 (Mick Woollett).

Bill Lomas (left) and Dickie Dale (right), two British racers with MV rides in the early days. This picture of Lomas was taken at Imola in 1972 (Mick Woollett).

blow for MV, who afterwards fell back on Italian riders to pursue the 500 cc championship—Bandirola, Masetti, Pagani and Forconi. None the less, the Spanish opening round gave hope as Bandirola and Masetti finished second and third, but the Gileras of Reg Armstrong and Geoffrey Duke were to prove too powerful and MV's lone 500 cc victory came in the final grand prix of the season at Monza, with Masetti running home ahead of Armstrong and Duke. Gilera again took the title and also secured second place, with Masetti occupying third position, 13 points behind the leader.

The opening 250 cc round that year was on the Isle of Man and although both Dickie Dale and Bill Lomas had left MV to join Guzzi at the end of 1954, Lomas accepted the offer to ride the new lighter 204 cc machine in the TT. He won in splendid style, moving MV off to a magnificent start in the class. 'It was a very good machine and quicker than the works 350 cc AJS', said Bill. His race average was 71.37 mph and he also set the fastest lap at 73.13 mph. It was after this success, reported Bill recently, that Count Agusta wanted him back to ride MVs in other classes, but on this

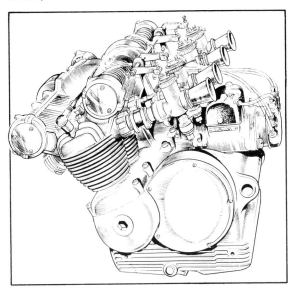

Above *MV's 1953 version of the transverse dohc four. Later versions, from 1956, started MV's impressive catalogue of victories and were succeeded by the three-cylinder machines (Drawing by Bill Bennett by courtesy of* Motor Cycle News).

25

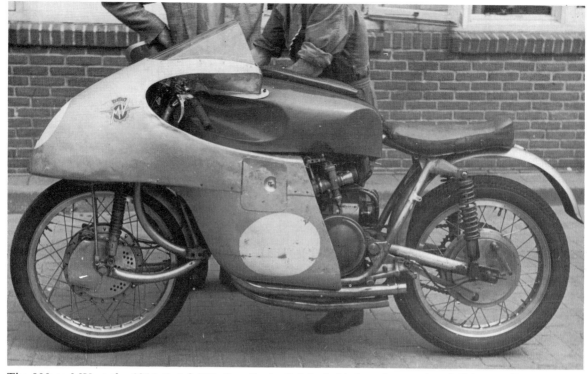

The 500 cc MV at the 1954 Dutch TT. Bandirola finished third at the meeting (Mick Woollett).

basis Lomas was not to be tempted, though he continued to ride during the remainder of the season in the 250 cc class. 'A blank sheet of paper was laid on the table and I could have put down my own price', revealed Bill. But by this time Lomas sensed he was in with a strong chance of honours riding the Guzzi in 350 cc racing and with four outright wins to come was destined to take the 350 cc world title that year, though in the opening round he was beaten into second place by a young Italian unknown called Agostini, though not Giacomo!

In Holland Lomas again took the new MV across the line first, but an international jury later relegated him to second place in favour of team mate Taveri for taking on fuel without stopping his engine. Even so, MV were proving quite a force in this class and in Holland occupied the first three places through Taveri, Lomas and Masetti. However, their challenge was not strong enough to take the individual title, which was won somewhat surprisingly by Hermann-Peter Muller of Germany on a factory-prepared single-cylinder production NSU Sportmax racer. Bill Lomas actually tied on

points with Muller and would have taken the title but for his downgrading at Assen.

In the 125 cc class, with the NSUs out of competition, MV had an easy ride and for the first time they dominated the class, winning all six grands prix. Ubbiali had an outstanding season, winning in France, the Isle of Man, Germany, Holland and Italy, and finishing third in the opening round in Spain. It was a performance which brought MV their second 125 cc world title and MV machines ridden by Taveri and Venturi were second and third.

A second individual World Championship, plus manufacturers world titles in both the 125 and 250 cc classes, were certainly worth having, but for all MV's effort in 1955 with the 500 machines, they had little to show. Here they still seemed short of rider talent.

As in 1949, when he signed Les Graham, the Count had been looking once more to Britain. For 1956 he approached a young Englishman named John Surtees. John signed for MV: a new, vibrant chapter in MV racing history was about to be written.

Chapter 4

Surtees signs—and more world titles

Bill Webster ran a motor cycle dealership in Crewe during the 1950s and '60s and, in his younger days, was also an enthusiastic racer. He and Les Graham used to meet casually at race meetings and, when Les moved to Italy after signing for MV, Bill visited the Graham family there and became quite a friend. In his racing days, Webster was a fanatically keen 'privateer', concentrating on the 125 and 250 cc classes. He was also a shrewd businessman with a sharp eye for the main chance and in the early 1950s, when a 125 cc MV was the thing to have, Bill managed to get hold of one of the production racers which Count Agusta put out at that time. He recognised the commercial value of these machines and became a kind of unofficial MV dealer in the UK. He was indeed the first man in Britain to race the early 125 cc MV. Though he did not have a works contract he visited the MV factory

periodically and later built up quite a relationship with Count Agusta, bringing to the notice of MV prospective British riders. Bill died from a heart attack suffered while watching a British race meeting in the mid-1960s, but he comes dramatically into the story at this point because it was through him that John Surtees was given his big chance with MV.

John had won the Ulster Grand Prix on a 250 cc NSU in 1955, after which he was invited to Monza to support the German factory's only works rider for that season, Hermann Muller, in the Italian classic. He produced some good times in practice, but a seized piston put him out of the running on race day. Bill Webster was there, as also was John's father, Jack Surtees, who was a prominent sidecar racer of his day and a contemporary and friend of Bill Webster. It was after one of John's practice

MV's Lightweight race team of 1957, left to right—Carlo Ubbiali (in dark glasses), Roberto Colombo and Luigi Taveri. Seen at the rear, between Colombo and Taveri, is the late Bill Webster (B.R. Nicholls).

sessions that Bill took both John Surtees and his father over to nearby Gallarate to meet Count Agusta, who was looking for someone to replace the ill-fated Ray Amm in the MV works team.

At that time John Surtees was already a rider of world class. After successful outings on Manx Nortons he was invited to join the Norton works team in 1955 and had an impressive season on the 'over the counter' factory racers. At British short circuits he had become something of a superstar, being adopted by the crowds at Brands Hatch as their unofficial 'king'. John was a dedicated and ambitious rider and it was becoming clear by 1955 that if he was to go after a World Championship seriously, it would be necessary to move from Norton. The writing was on the wall for the once proud factory and the retirement of Joe Craig, their extremely clever chief development engineer and team manager, seemed to put the final seal, symbolically at any rate, on their racing demise.

Gilera were also showing interest in Surtees, but Bill Webster's arrangement for John and his father to meet Count Agusta was definite. The visitors were received cordially, shown the machines and given a tour of the race shop. Following Webster's recommendation, Domenico offered Surtees an immediate contract and after first confirming with Norton's managing director, Gilbert Smith, that there could be no racing future for him with the old firm (Norton had decided against supporting the championship races in 1956), and checking that MVs were machines which he would be happy to ride, Surtees decided to accept the Italian offer.

Riding MV machinery over the next five years John Surtees was to become the biggest name in motor cycle racing. Together he and MV created one of the most vibrant and sparkling periods of the company's entire history.

At the time Surtees signed up it was not everyone's ambition to climb aboard the Italian factory's machines. The memories of Les Graham's and Ray Amm's fatal crashes and the succession of spills by their native rider Carlo Bandirola, had raised some doubts about the handling of the bikes at speed and led a number of people to warn Surtees against the move. But he was not superstitious. Nor foolhardy, for he decided to test the machines thoroughly before committing himself.

He was impressed by the engines, but found too much movement in the frame. He agreed that with this rectified he would ride the MVs during 1956. John tried the machines at Monza and Modena. At Monza he lapped repeatedly at 1 min 58/59 secs on an unstreamlined machine—and on a muddy, wet

MV's formidable line-up for 1956. From left to right: John Surtees, Umberto Masetti, Carlo Ubbiali, Carlo Bandirola, Count Domenico Agusta, Angelo Copeta, Remo Venturi, Luigi Taveri and Tito Forconi. Not pictured, but also in the team, was Lightweight-only rider Fortunato Libanori (Mick Woollett).

The machine which brought John Surtees his first MV Isle of Man victory in 1956, in the Senior TT (Mick Woollett).

surface covered with leaves. This was only four seconds slower than the fastest lap raced in the Italian Grand Prix the previous September. At Modena his fastest lap was only one second outside the lap record.

Count Augsta was delighted and handed out a long term contract for Surtees to ride 350 and 500 cc MVs in World Championship races and in selected internationals.

The Count had decided on a massive offensive for 1956 and was to contest all four solo classes with a crop of top riders. Supporting Surtees in the heavier classes would be Umberto Masetti and Carlo Bandirola, with Tito Forconi as reserve. Carlo Ubbiali led the lightweight team which included Remo Venturi, Luigi Taveri and Angelo Copeta. Nello Pagani had been appointed team manager, in an example typical of the Italian approach of the day where the test rider and development engineer worked in the race shop and acted as a kind of semi-team manager.

In spite of his powerful offensive in terms of riders and classes in which MV would compete, the MV machinery witnessed little significant change from 1955. What change there was came from the

efforts of Surtees: a comparatively modest redesign of the frame and improved maximum power output and torque in the medium rpm range. The 500 was a better machine for 1956 and even more competitive. The 52 mm × 58 mm engine was capable of about 150 mph on the right circuit and gave about 65 bhp at some 10,500 rpm. The Earles forks had been exchanged for telescopics. It looked a fair prospect, even against the skill and power of Geoffrey Duke on the Gilera, but in the 350 cc class Guzzi were likely to continue to have the edge against an MV which was somewhat too heavy. John took an instant liking to Arturo Magni and he welcomed the enthusiasm and helpful attitude of the mechanics.

His competitive baptism with MV could not have been better. He won his first two races at Crystal Palace and then two more at Silverstone. Domenico took the results as a good omen and sent off his team to the Isle of Man full of hope and enthusiasm. MV had not contested the TTs until 1951, but in 1956 they almost created a sensation. Only cruel luck robbed the factory of a Senior/Junior TT double. Surtees was all set to take the Junior race when, with only a quarter of a lap to go, his engine failed and the machine was out of petrol. This serious error in refuelling stranded him on the mountain and cost him the race. He took on petrol from a spectator and was disqualified for so doing. He made no such mistake in the Senior and rode to victory at a race average of 96.57 mph, with a fastest lap at 97.79 mph. Except for Geoffrey Duke's 97.93 mph the previous year, the MV's race average was faster than anything before.

In the second round in Holland, MV scored a fine victory in the 500 cc race and were second in the 350 cc event. Surtees had a comfortable win in the former after an early challenge from the fuel injected BMW of Walter Zeller and broke the race and lap records set up by Geoffrey Duke the previous year. In the Junior event, an inspired Bill Lomas on the Guzzi had a great ride and Surtees just could not get the MV in front.

A great deal of excitement which surrounded John Surtees' signing for MV had stemmed from the close rivalry that existed between the MV and Gilera factories. With the decline of Norton, racing's foremost rider, Geoffrey Duke, had signed for Gilera and had brought them the 500 cc World Championship for the previous three years. At 22 years of age, Surtees was accepted as the rising young star and, as already mentioned, had conquered the British short circuit scene before moving to MV. The anticipated clash between Duke and Surtees, Gilera and MV, had brought a new dimension to the series. Or it should have done. The disappointment was that Duke, along with Gilera team mate Reg Armstrong, were sidelined in the early part of the season because of their part in supporting private riders who had refused to ride in the Dutch TT in 1955 as a protest against not being paid enough start money.

The clash between MV and Gilera had to be postponed until the next round in Belgium. Duke was out of suspension by now and keen to show that the Gilera was still the better machine. Surtees would be riding with the confidence that only maximum points from two championship races out of two could give.

According to Surtees' recollection of the race, practice times had shown how difficult it was going to be for the MVs to hold the Gilera, the latter with modified ratios to incorporate a special fourth gear which was to be used for the long uphill stretch from Stavelot. From the start, Surtees took the MV to the front and held the lead for five laps. Then the Gilera roared past and Surtees was faced with having to decide whether to run the risk of taking off in pursuit and possibly over-revving the MV or to settle for second place and six valuable championship points. He had virtually decided on

the latter tactic—perhaps most sensibly—when the unlucky Duke had to retire with valve trouble on the 13th lap.

That day in Belgium during the summer of 1956 was one of jubilation for Count Agusta and his entire team, for MVs were raced to victory in all the four solo classes, a record at that time. Surtees won the 350 cc race to complete the double and Ubbiali won the 125 cc and 250 cc events, with Taveri second in both races.

As the MV team prepared to move to Solitude for the German Grand Prix, their position in the World Championships had never been stronger. Ubbiali had mopped up in the 125 and 250 cc classes, winning all six races in the Isle of Man, Holland and Belgium. Surtees led in the 350 cc and 500 cc categories. In the latter his position looked impregnable. He had 24 points against the 14 amassed by his nearest rival, Walter Zeller. With the championship being decided on the best four performances out of six races, he needed just one more win to clinch the title. Less comfortably placed in the 350 cc class, Surtees still led by five points from August Hobl on a DKW machine and the wily Bill Lomas on the ever-threatening Guzzi.

It does not do to anticipate too much in racing, as MV were soon to learn. In the 350 cc race Surtees started confidently, taking the bike to the front of the pack with Bill Lomas screaming close behind. But Lomas took the lead after a lap or two and began edging away. He was riding beautifully and cracked the lap record at 93.53 mph. Then Surtees began to close the distance and on lap seven was only inches away. He rushed the bike into one of the bends and, in a fraction of a second, MV's dreams were shattered. The front wheel shuddered and slipped on loose sand. The machine spun out of control and Surtees was thrust across the road, hit the bank and lost consciousness. He was taken to hospital in Stuttgart and, although he was lucky not to be more badly hurt, the crash had robbed MV of any chance of taking a double world title.

Surtees, with a badly broken and bruised arm (which later had to be permanently pinned), was out of action for the remainder of the season and he had a nail-biting time waiting to see if Bill Lomas, who was now favourite for the 350 cc championship, would secure enough points to overhaul him. Lomas had gone on to win in Germany and in Belfast and, with only the Monza round outstanding, confirmed his form with another fine win from team mate Dickie Dale on the Guzzi.

However, in the 500 cc championship MV took the title for the very first time, for Surtees had done enough in the first three rounds before his crash to finish eight points clear of his nearest challenger, Walter Zeller on a BMW.

It was a year in which MV carried off three individual world titles and their machines had done so well that they had gained the manufacturers award in three out of the four classes contested— Guzzi in the 350 cc category denying them 100 per cent recognition. Carlo Ubbiali had been in a class of his own on the MV in the 125 and 250 cc classes. In 12 races during the year in both categories, this superbly skilled rider was unbeaten in 11. Taveri helped to make it a highly successful season for MV by finishing second in the 250 cc class and third in the 125 cc class.

With three world titles in 1956 there was every reason for Count Agusta to look forward with confidence to 1957, but the fluctuations of racing once again stepped in to take a hand. Just as MV might have considered they were beginning to overhaul the opposition, their morale was shattered not only by their great rival Gilera, but also by Mondial. The season was to prove that the smaller MVs were not as fast as the new Mondials and that, in spite of all their efforts, the MV mechanics still had not produced a machine to match the Gilera,

for all the latter's undependable handling. Surtees' crippled arm was a long time mending and the World Champion was not able to get in as many rides as he would have liked before the season began. Even so, he won a running battle with team mate Carlo Bandirola during the opening grand prix in Spain and, in doing so, ran the gauntlet of the MV camp. They would have preferred Bandirola to take the race, had it come to a choice, for a victory by the dashing Italian, who was a favourite at Montjuich Park, would have been most popular. But Surtees would have none of it and the two team mates became race rivals as first Surtees raced ahead, then pulled back to let Bandirola gain ground, before racing ahead once more.

It was a deliberate tactic on Surtees' part for his arm troubled him badly and he felt desperately tired after about three laps. So his plan was to blast ahead for three laps, ease back for three and then rush ahead once more. In the end Surtees cleverly outfoxed the Italian. Towards the end of the race, as Surtees slowed down for what Bandirola thought would be the customary three laps, the British rider blasted ahead with full acceleration after only half a lap and Bandirola, realising he had been caught

The 1957 vintage MV four (B.R. Nicholls).

napping, raced in pursuit but overdid things and crashed into a tree. Surtees went on to win without trouble.

The second round of the series was the Isle of Man TT but mechanical problems in the Junior event and a tactical miscalculation in the Senior robbed MV of victory. Surtees' fourth position in the Junior race was largely because of plug trouble which meant two extravagant pit stops. In the Senior, with the forecasters predicting gusty conditions, it was decided that Surtees should ride the MV without its streamlining. The conditions turned out to be perfect and the naked MV was no match for the streamlined Gilera of Bob McIntyre. It was in this race that the great Scottish rider cracked the 100 mph lap barrier for the first time. Surtees brought the MV home a couple of minutes later.

Although in Holland, in the next round, Surtees romped home at record speed in the 500 cc race, suspension problems forced his retirement in the 350 cc event and in the Belgium Grand Prix the following week, the MVs had to be retired with piston trouble in both races. This really scuttled any chance MV might have had to retain the 500 cc crown. In the Ulster Grand Prix the MV pushed the lap record to 95.69 mph before piston trouble once more forced Surtees' withdrawal. In the final round at Monza it was engine trouble which relegated the MV to fourth position after Surtees had scrapped excitingly with Gilera's Liberati for half the race.

It was obvious at Monza that the Count had been concerned at the season's dismal showing and Pagani was given a new 500 six to try out in practice, but it was not raced.

MV, who in 1956 stormed the racing world by taking three out of the four solo World Championships, were left with nothing in 1957. They did not even gain a manufacturers award. With beautifully streamlined double overhead camshaft single-cylinder machines, Mondial had sensationally overhauled them in the 125 and 250 cc classes, where even the outstanding skills of Carlo Ubbiali were insufficient to bridge the gap. Guzzi, through Keith Campbell, gained the 350 cc title and the Italian rider, Libero Liberati, took Gilera to the top honours in the 500 cc category.

Although the results table made sorry reading for Count Agusta and the MV team, there was by the end of the season renewed hope in their camp. Surtees had made it known earlier in the season that he was far from happy with the handling of the MV

fours at speed and wanted Count Agusta to rubber-stamp a change of fork design. Nothing changed until Surtees, after his retirements in Belgium, confronted the Count with a rough drawing of what he thought would be an improved fork and also some suggestions for a new frame layout. With the new forks Surtees maintained the machine handled better in Belfast and again at Monza. So MV could look forward with a little more hope to the 1958 season, particularly since a vast amount of work was done during the winter to eliminate the mechanical problems the machines had suffered in 1957.

During the winter MV sustained a hectic programme of experiment and testing, trying different pistons and valve springs in a concerted effort to eliminate the mechanical problems that had been their undoing in '57. There was also a new duplex frame which Surtees had largely built himself. John reckoned that for 1958 the 500 machine was performing really well and that it would have been a match for anything Gilera could have produced. Unfortunately, the battle of these two Italian giants was destined never to take place, for at this critical point, Gilera, along with Guzzi and Mondial, decided that racing for grand prix honour was too expensive and they quit.

The year was particularly significant from the mechanical point of view for the machine which Surtees rode in 1956 remained, with only detail modifications to the frame and streamlining, until 1960. The twin overhead camshafts were driven by a gear train placed between the inner cylinders, there was a five-speed gear box and a Lucas magneto. The handling was much improved with the telescopic forks at the front. At the rear the tubular duplex frame had a swinging-fork suspension of conventional design, with chain final drive. The bike's brief specifications were:

Engine	Four-in-line mounted transversely 500 cc dohc drive to camshafts by gear train between inboard cylinders and four carburettors.
Ignition	Lucas magneto.
Transmission	Gear primary drive to five-speed gearbox and final drive by chain.
Frame	Duplex cradle with pivoting-fork rear suspension.
Forks	Telescopic.

Chapter 5

MV take over the world

With their three major rivals no longer racing there was little to oppose the works MVs in the three years from 1958. In one of the most remarkable runs of success in the entire history of World Championship competition, MV took all four solo world titles in all three years. The record was sensational. The flying MV machines smashed numerous race and lap records and of the 76 World Championship races held in all four solo classes during those three years, MVs were first home on all except 13 occasions—some of those because the championships had been wrapped up and the Count did not even bother to send his team; or because he could miss a round or two and still be confident of the title.

Critics will point out that the championships were easy game for MV during those three years. Certainly, the withdrawal of Gilera, Guzzi and Mondial left them with a much clearer field, but John Surtees believes that at the beginning of 1958 he and the mechanics had done a lot to cure the mechanical and handling problems which had beset the bigger machines and he regretted the absence of the major works challengers. It is also true that the Nortons and AJSs in 1958 were considerably faster than they had been, Geoff Duke was a potential menace on a works BMW and, on the Isle of Man, Bob McIntyre, on Joe Potts' Nortons, could never be discounted.

For the 1958 season John Hartle had been recruited to the MV team and rode in the heavier classes as team mate to Surtees. After a comparatively easy win in Spain, the MV contingent travelled to the Isle of Man. In the Junior race Surtees led all the way and won at an average speed of 93.97 mph, while Hartle retired with piston failure. In the Senior race, Geoff Duke and Bob McIntyre were seen as the leading challengers to the MVs, but Duke went out after only one lap. McIntyre, after a sensational start from which he split the MVs of Surtees and Hartle and almost clocked the first 100 mph lap on a Norton, retired with engine trouble. On the fourth of the seven laps the MVs looked comfortable with Surtees and Hartle in first and second positions, but as he came out of the slow hairpin at Governor's Bridge, Hartle's machine caught fire.

Surtees' double success on the Isle of Man was the prelude to an astonishing period of racing. In Holland, Belgium, Germany, Northern Ireland and Italy Surtees raced the MVs to 350 and 500 cc 'doubles' to gain six successive doubles victories in six meetings. He secured both World Championships with maximum points. Only in Sweden, included in the championship round for the first time in 1958, were the MVs absent from the winners lists and that was because by then Surtees had made sure of both championships and Count Agusta decided it was not worth the expense of sending Surtees and Hartle to compete.

In the 125 and 250 cc classes, MVs had a slightly harder run. Count Agusta retained the services of Carlo Ubbiali, the world's best rider of lighter machines, and he and Tarquinio Provini together

March 1958, and a youthful-looking John Surtees is seen with the ill-fated six-cylinder 500 cc MV during tests at Monza. The machine was never to be developed successfully (Mick Woollett).

won eight of the 13 championship rounds. Ubbiali, with wins on the Isle of Man, Holland, Germany and Northern Ireland, took the 125 cc title, while Provini was victorious on the Isle of Man and in Holland, Germany and Northern Ireland to finish as 250 cc World Champion.

For the Monza meeting the Italian factories had always been keen to do something special and, although MV had the stage virtually to themselves in 1958, it did not prevent them from bringing out an experimental six-cylinder machine for the 500 cc race. Work had started on this bike during the winter and both Surtees and Hartle had tried it out before the new season. MV might have developed it with more urgency, but with the threat of the eight-cylinder Guzzi and the Gilera removed for 1958, Count Agusta fell back on the MV fours. But the interest that had accompanied the six-cylinder machine's appearance was not maintained, for Hartle, who rode it in the race at Monza, had to retire after a few laps because the machine developed engine trouble.

How do you improve on four World Championships out of four contested in one season? That was MV's challenge for 1959 and if, for some critics, grand prix racing was becoming banal and was losing much of its fire because of the MV superiority, there is no denying that a works team, however much above the opposition, adds that ultimate dimension to championship racing which is inevitably absent no matter how close non-works

Above *In 1958 Tarquinio Provini brought MV their second individual 250 cc World Championship. He is seen racing to victory in the Ulster Grand Prix that year at an average speed of 77.41 mph. He also recorded the fastest lap at 80.71 mph* (B.R. Nicholls).

Below *MV's rider talent for 1958 (left to right) Nello Pagani (team manager) Fortunato Libanori, John Hartle, Remo Venturi, Tarquinio Provini, Count Domenico Agusta, Carlo Ubbiali, Gilberto Milani, Ernesto Brambilla and John Surtees* (Mick Woollett).

The Ulster Grand Prix of 1958 and John Hartle hurtles the 500 cc MV four at 84.5 mph to finish third behind Surtees and McIntyre (B.R. Nicholls).

entries might be. It can be argued that the World Championships need that extra-special something which only factory involvement can provide and without it the championships lose much of the glamour, excitement and status for which they were intended.

In the 125 cc class the challenge from Ducati waned and although Gary Hocking's form on a new MZ in the 250 cc class worried Count Agusta—he even beat Ubbiali in Sweden and won again in the Ulster Grand Prix—MVs finally took the honours. Surtees was again supreme in both 350 and 500 cc racing and MV ended the season with four more World Championships, their riders also occupying runner-up positions in all four solo classes.

There was a personal milestone at stake for John Surtees on the Isle of Man. In the 48 year history of the TT races, only the legendary Stanley Woods had ridden to Junior and Senior success in two successive years (1932 and '33). In 1959 Surtees had the chance of equalling that record with the MVs.

The prospects looked good as the MV romped home in the Junior race, with Surtees putting up new lap records at 95.38 mph and 97.08 mph. On the Friday of TT week, traditionally the Senior day, the weather enforced a postponement for 24 hours and the race took place on the Saturday. The extra power of the works MVs gave little chance to the non-works entries in good conditions, but counted for less in poor weather and, although Gary Hocking had been forced to leave the island for a racing commitment in Sweden, Bob McIntyre on a Norton was still a major threat and was generally at his best on the Isle of Man.

Surtees recalls the race as the coldest and most uncomfortable he had ever ridden. Despite worsening conditions, the MV set the fastest lap at 101.18 mph the first time round. John Hartle on the second MV was chasing Surtees, but the weather, now incorporating near gale force wind, was picking off its victims—Dickie Dale, Mike Hailwood and then John Hartle, who crashed and was carted off to hospital suffering from concussion. Alastair King on a Norton now became the MV's nearest rival and McIntyre, whose position had suffered because of a malfunctioning clutch, was hauling himself up and on the fifth lap moved from 12th to 7th in a fine display of riding in the rain. Although the bad weather cut down the times, Surtees won and the double was his.

In the 500 cc class Surtees and the MV had a magnificent season. He not only won all seven World Championship rounds, but set up new records in every race—even in the TT's miserable conditions when his fastest lap of 101.18 mph was faster than any rider had gone round the TT circuit before. Probably the most interesting encounters involving the MV during the remainder of the 1959 season were in the Ulster and Italian Grands Prix towards the end of the season.

Until Surtees had emerged as the new champion, Geoffrey Duke had been the darling of the circuits with his polished, controlled style of riding and, for a number of years, the most keenly hoped for situation in the 500 cc class was a race on equal terms between Duke and Surtees. Finally to seal such an encounter, Duke should ideally have been on the Gilera and Surtees on the MV but, unfortunately, this battle of the giants was never realised because of, first, Duke's suspension and, later, Surtees' injury.

Nevertheless, in 1959 Duke took what were reputed to be two remarkably fast Nortons to Belfast to face the combined might of MV and Surtees. The former champion was said still to be riding with considerable skill and flair, and on the tough, winding Dundrod circuit, the extra power of the MV could not be used to the same advantage as on a more open circuit like, for instance, Francochamps in Belgium. In the 350 cc race there was an impressive entry which included Mike Hailwood and Bob McIntyre, both on AJS machines. Surtees moved into the lead from the start, with McIntyre in second place and Hartle on the second MV well down the field, but John stormed through and moved into third place behind McIntyre in lap three. On the fourth lap Hartle's massive effort to overtake McIntyre was successful. Then, on the seventh lap and after shattering the record with a lap at 93.35 mph, he crashed after touching the banking and was out of the race. As Surtees raced on to win, establishing a new race average at 91.32 mph, the battle with Duke never looked like developing and the former champion finished in third place behind Bob Brown on a Norton.

The real clash was anticipated in the 500 cc event but, sadly for the race fans, it did not materialise there either. Surtees' MV was much the superior machine in the race and he romped home ahead of Duke, who finished third after McIntyre. It was a similar story at Monza in the last grand prix of the season. Surtees and Remo Venturi, now MV

The start of the 250 cc race at the Dutch TT in 1959. Provini (2) and Ubbiali (1) were to finish first and second (Mick Woollett).

mounted, finished first and second in the 350 cc race and repeated the placings in the 500 cc event, when Surtees shattered the Monza lap record at 119.11 mph. It was a sweet record for Count Agusta, for it robbed his keen rival and near neighbour, Gilera, of the honour. Their star rider, Libero Liberati, had taken the record there in 1957 at 118 mph.

Any victory over Gilera was particularly welcomed by Count Agusta because the rivalry between the two neighbouring Italian factories had always been keen. It is disappointing from this angle that Gilera had to disappear from racing when they did, because the MV by 1958 was becoming a much more capable machine and would have given them many close battles. The tension which existed between the two was perhaps not altogether surprising. Gilera had led the multi-cylinder march against the single-cylinder domination of the British factories and had taken the 500 cc title four years running when MV came along. They had a long tradition, both as a motor cycle manufacturer and in racing. MV, in sharp contrast, had no tradition and little experience and had not been in racing for more than a handful of years. Domenico's early recruitment of Remor had not helped to sweeten relations between the two factories and was accentuated by a kind of indigenous rivalry, in the traditional Italian mould, between the two local aristocratic families.

There was always that additional excitement when Gilera and MV came to the starting line together and the antagonism sometimes broke the surface for others to witness. Bill Lomas is among a number of riders who remember MV's sensational win at Monza in 1952 when Les Graham finished ahead of the Gileras of Masetti and Pagani. Not since the championships had been reconstituted in 1949 had Gilera been beaten in the class at Monza by an Italian factory, their only other defeat coming in 1950 at the hands of Geoffrey Duke and Norton. They were so incensed that they lodged a protest and had the winning MV measured. Domenico responded by putting in a counter protest and insisted that the second and third placed Gileras be measured!

During these years of total MV domination, Surtees took most of the spotlight. As premier rider in the most glamorous 350 and 500 cc races it was inevitable, if unfortunate, that this record should obscure some impressive riding of the MV by that outstanding British rider John Hartle. He spent two years with the firm and, although in too many races he crashed or was frustrated through mechanical breakdown, he did finish second to Surtees in nine World Championship races.

Provini with the 250 cc MV twin at Assen in July 1959 (Mick Woollett).

Hartle had made his big-time debut at Scarborough in 1954 and it was at the same circuit 14 years later that his career was tragically ended when he crashed fatally. In those 14 years he had works rides for Norton and Gilera as well as MV and came nearest to a world title in 1967 when he finished second on a Matchless in the 500 cc World Championship. In 1956 he won his first classic in Ulster on a Norton. John Surtees, who had been a team mate of Hartle in the Norton works team of 1955, considered him a rider of outstanding talent. When, at the end of 1956, Count Agusta asked Surtees to recommend another rider for the MV team, John's first choice was Hartle. Not generally known was that Bob McIntyre was also a candidate for the vacant works place. He became first choice when it was understood that Hartle's commitments at the time might have prevented him from spending as much time as was necessary on the Continent. It seemed certain that the talented Scot would sign for MV as Surtees and Bill Webster approached McIntyre with a contract at an end-of-season meeting in Britain. But just when it seemed that Bob

In 1959 Carlo Ubbiali brought MV the 125 and 250 cc World Championships. Here he is seen riding the 125 cc machine (Mick Woollett).

was to become an MV team rider, there came the shock news that he had signed for the rival Gilera team.

Hartle's two years with MV were not very happy or satisfactory. Playing second fiddle to Surtees must have become irritating and when he missed races through injury his reputation with Count Agusta was further damaged. Their relationship became strained towards the end of 1959 and in 1960 Hartle quit the Italian factory and started racing his own Nortons. By that time Gary Hocking, who had been a nuisance to Count Agusta because of his superb riding of the remarkably fast MZ in the 250 cc class in 1959, had joined the MV team, though ironically Hartle's final fling with MV brought what were perhaps his best results—a fine first and second in the Junior and Senior TTs and a second place in the 350 cc Ulster Grand Prix. He also retained the distinction of being the only rider to race the 500 cc MV six, when it broke down in the 1958 Italian Grand Prix.

*　　*　　*

Critics who belittled MV's racing record in 1958 and '59 because of the dearth of serious opposition, perhaps never realised how close they had come at

the end of 1957 to facing the infinitely more dismal alternative. Racing without Gilera, Guzzi and Mondial was bad enough. Without MV's continued presence the World Championships would surely have been much the poorer. Disappointing though their departure may have been to race fans, the disappearance of Gilera from the European circuits was not altogether surprising. Their early world-beating fours were developed only after a vast amount of research and expenditure which, as a fairly small company, they could ill afford. Perhaps, therefore, it was commercially right to call a halt at that time. Guzzi, too, with their fine tradition of technical brilliance, must have invested large sums over the many years they supported racing, while Mondial, for all their success, would have found the considerable investment necessary to keep ahead in racing difficult to justify.

The combined retirements of Gilera, Guzzi and Mondial—which were said to have shocked their own team riders as much as anyone else because they had no prior knowledge of the dramatic decision—were really a concerted protest against the growing and crippling costs of World Championship racing. The FIM had been under heavy pressure to do something about it, perhaps by limiting the formula, and for a time MV's position

38

was also in the balance. When the FIM seemed reluctant to move, the pulling out of the three major factories might well have been a defiant demonstration of strength. Could the World Championships survive without their support? For a time the whole structure of grand prix racing seemed in the balance, but when it became clear that the FIM were determined that the series should go ahead as planned in 1958, even without the support of some of the biggest names, the World Championships were there for the picking and Count Agusta shrewdly decided to continue.

It was a time of change as, following numerous accidents, the FIM banned the use of full streamlining and ruled out fairings which enclosed the front wheel of the machine or covered the rider. Though the Count's passion for racing was unquestionable, there was also a commercial reason for MV's continuing presence in the grand prix. For the next two years they used the race success of the 350 and 500 cc fours as a powerful argument to help sell the lightweight machines which formed the factory's production. It is a curious feature of MV that during this time of sensational success in racing, no larger capacity machines were produced for non-racing use.

It was another of MV's strict policies which partially decided John Surtees to retire from motor cycle racing after just one more season. The Count felt that he could obtain the greatest recognition by competing in the World Championships and just a few selected international races, so that Surtees was barred from taking the crowd-pulling MVs to a number of meetings at which he would have preferred to be present. This, combined with the lack of opposition to the MVs and the fact that there seemed little left to be won after a couple of double World Championships and TTs, accelerated Surtees' transition to motor racing.

However, 1960 would bring him the chance to improve on the distinction he shared with Stanley Woods: it would also give him the opportunity to become the first rider in history to win the Junior-Senior TT double in three successive seasons.

As it turned out, it was an ambition he failed to realise and the man who denied Surtees a three-times TT double was none other than his old friend and team mate John Hartle. The Junior TT was Surtees' bogey race. He moved off well enough and on the opening lap set a new class record at 98.26 mph. His second lap was even better at 99.20 mph, but then mechanical problems robbed him of any chance of a triple Senior-Junior double. He lost bottom gear, then fourth gear and, towards the end of the race, the engine lacked a good deal of

compression. In the meantime, Hartle hurtled on and took the lead on the fifth lap and won at a record average for the race of 96.70 mph.

In the Senior race Surtees urged the MV ahead from the start and cracked the existing lap record with a speed of 103.03 mph. The two MVs were again leading the race and on the second lap Surtees pushed the record to 104.08 mph. He improved the distance between himself and Hartle and won at a race record average of 102.44 mph.

Surtees' consolation in not beating Stanley Woods' 'double' record came in being the first rider to win the Senior TT three times running. He also equalled Stanley Woods' record of winning the race four times.

At Clermont Ferrand in the opening round Gary Hocking had taken the 350 cc race for MV while Surtees had been first home in the 500 cc event, but in Holland, immediately after the TTs, John turned the tables on Hocking and beat him to first place in the 350 at a record average of 83.53 mph. He was out of luck in the 500 cc race, however, and after repeated stops because of engine trouble he came off and had to retire. Remo Venturi, however, kept the MV flag flying with a fine win from Bob Brown on a Norton. Poor John Hartle, rapidly losing favour, had been dropped from the MV team to contest Holland.

A record lap of 122.67 mph and a record race average of 120.53 mph took Surtees and MV to victory in the 500 cc event in Belgium, where there was no 350 cc class. MV did well again in the German Grand Prix at Solitude, Surtees, Venturi and Mendogni occupying the first three places in the 500 cc race. Again there was no 350 cc round in Germany, but the meeting was saddened by the death of Bob Brown, who crashed on a 250 cc Honda while practising.

At the Ulster Grand Prix, Surtees' 350 cc win made certain that he would once again be a double World Champion. It was a remarkable achievement. Surtees had now taken the double title three years in succession—the first rider to accomplish such a deed in the 11 years' history of the championships. John Surtees ended his racing days with MV and his motor cycle career at Monza at the end of 1960 by winning the 500 cc race and retiring in the 350 cc event.

His epic battle with John Hartle in the 500 cc race of the Ulster during this final year is still vividly remembered. After moving into an early lead, with Alan Shepherd on a Matchless in second place and John Hartle on a Norton lying third, the gear on the MV broke on the second lap and Surtees was left to ease the machine back to the pits in low gear and there to have a new gear lever fitted. It took the mechanics a long time to complete the repairs and by the time he was able to rejoin the race, he faced a monumental task. Bob McIntyre was now in the lead, with a field of tremendous talent in pursuit— Hailwood, Shepherd, Redman and then Hartle. Surtees was down in 42nd position with a hopeless task before him. With 18 laps to go and a full three minutes in arrears, John rejoined the race.

He was fortunate that McIntyre had to retire with machine vibration and Hailwood endured an over-long stay at the pits while an ignition fault was put right. Hartle now surged into the lead with Surtees a long, long way behind. Relentlessly, he closed the distance and, breaking the lap record time and again, he only just failed to catch Hartle. It was a remarkable demonstration of rider courage and determination and also said much for the MV which did well to withstand such relentless pressure.

There was now little left for Surtees to win in motor cycle racing. He had become increasingly attracted to a career on four wheels, but it was also his disagreement with Count Agusta over the latter's policy of not permitting his contracted riders to race in other events, even on their own

Another MV victory for Ubbiali. On the victors rostrum at the famous Hockenheim circuit in 1959, when he won both 125 and 250 cc races. MV won every race there that year, Surtees taking the 350 and 500 cc events (Mick Woollett).

machinery, which helped to make up his mind. As Surtees commented afterwards: 'I could understand his reasons for wanting to save the four-cylinder machines for the championship races, but could never understand why he objected to his riders using their own machines in other races'. One reason, of course, would have been the risk of injury to the rider.

For the third successive year MV had won all four classes in the World Championships and, at the end of 1960, their record was quite phenomenal. In just ten years serious racing they had secured 17 individual World Championships and won 82 classic races, not to mention 19 manufacturers world titles!

Such sweeping success might suggest that Surtees had an easy passage. Certainly, with Gilera in the field it would have been harder, but John's contribution to MV was none the less enormous. The continuing development work initiated by him affecting the frame layout and suspension had made the MVs much better machines while the fours, even at their most respectful, needed a superior rider to get the best out of them.

However, 1960 was to be a turning point in a number of ways. John Hartle fell from favour and left MV. Surtees moved on to car racing. Carlo Ubbiali decided to retire. Gary Hocking signed for the factory. Perhaps the most significant development of all, however, had been the challenge to MV in the 125 cc and 250 cc classes by Honda, a relatively unknown factory from far-away Japan. Though there were no means of Count Agusta knowing, within just one year MV would be stripped of the 125 cc and 250 cc titles and in a further year would be left with only the 500 cc World Championship to their credit. Their long reign in the 500 cc class was to continue uninterrupted in the most outstanding run of success known in racing, but their monopoly of the lighter classes had gone: it was never to return.

* * *

In this final season of total domination by MV it is interesting to look at the men who helped to make the machines immortal. In the 125 cc class Ubbiali was the star rider, winning four of the five grands prix. He was supported by Taveri, Hocking and Spaggiari. In the 250 cc class, Ubbiali again was the top rider with four wins out of six races. Taveri and Hocking also figured in the results. Surtees, Hocking and Hartle took the MV honours in the 350 cc races. In the 500 cc class Surtees was, of course, supreme with Venturi doing well with a win in Holland and three second places. Italian rider Mendogni gained a second place in the Italian Grand Prix and a third in Germany.

Surtees had, in all, collected seven world titles, Ubbiali nine, and there is no doubt that had Carlo Ubbiali elected to leave the lighter machines for the heavier and more glamorous classes, he might well have been even more successful and gained even greater recognition. Without doubt, he was one of the most brilliant riders ever produced by Italy. He was an outstanding reader of a race, had a rare unity with his machinery, and his small frame made him ideal for riding the smaller bikes. With MV, Ubbiali did not always find the going easy. In the beginning the German NSUs were much superior to the MVs and even Ubbiali's brilliance could not make up the difference. In his later years with Count Agusta, he faced ever-increasing competition, especially from the remarkably fast East German MZ two-strokes. But he remained an exceptionally gifted rider and Count Agusta did well to have him for so long as a member of his team.

Ubbiali's considerable achievements with the smaller MVs tend to be overshadowed by Surtees' record on the more powerful bikes. His last appearance on the Isle of Man in 1960 brought him his fourth 125 cc TT victory. Over the Mountain circuit, preferred to the former Clypse Course, he led from start to finish at a race average of 85.60 mph and raised the lap record on the second of the three laps to 86.13 mph. These are the brief specifications of the 125 cc MV winner, which really was little changed from previous years:

Engine	Single-cylinder 125 cc dohc, drive to camshafts by gear train.
Ignition	Coil, with contact-breaker driven by skew gear from engine drive-side mainshaft.
Transmission	Gear primary drive to unit construction six-speed gear-box; final drive by chain.
Frame	Duplex cradle with pivoting-fork rear suspension.
Forks	Telescopic.

Born in Bergamo in 1929, Ubbiali was 20 when he began racing and was quickly spotted by Mondial, joining their works team in the 125 cc class. He stayed with Mondial for three years, winning his first World Championship in 1951 at 22 years of age. He was an outstanding tactician and his calm, untemperamental approach, unusual in an Italian, made him one of the most admired and

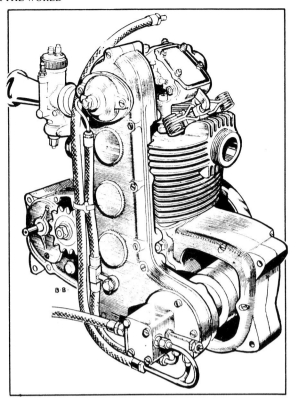

Beautifully crafted production 125 cc MV with massive casing enclosing the gear drive to the single overhead camshaft (Drawing by Bill Bennett courtesy of *Motor Cycle News).*

respected characters in the sport. He first appeared in the Isle of Man with Mondial in 1951, finishing second in the 125 cc race, but his first win there was with MV in 1955.

Luigi Taveri, born in Switzerland, was one of the finest road racers to come from that country. Although he raced MVs, and also Ducati machines, his greatest recognition came in the 1960s with Honda when he was 125 cc World Champion in 1962, '64 and '66. He was small, with an excellent racing style.

John Hartle was a courageous and dedicated rider and continued to race motor cycles in spite of a number of serious crashes. After his brief spell with MV he rode privately sponsored Nortons with mixed fortunes. A crash at Scarborough in 1961 put him out of racing for two years, but he made a comeback as a member of Geoffrey Duke's Gilera challenge team in 1963. He rode magnificently on the Isle of Man to take second place to Mike Hailwood in the Senior TT that year, lapping at 105.56 mph. He sustained a fractured skull in a crash at Imola in 1964 but was racing again, with

Above *Former Norton riders, John Hartle and John Surtees, discuss race tactics at the 1960 Ulster Grand Prix when riding for MV. They finished first (Surtees) and second in the 350 cc event and Hartle won the 500 cc race on a Norton (B.R. Nicholls).* **Below** *John Hartle racing the 350 cc MV four to victory in the 1960 Junior TT (B.R. Nicholls).*

The style of John Surtees, seen on the 350 cc MV four at Silverstone in April 1959 (B.R. Nicholls).

medical approval, two years later. He succeeded dramatically, winning at Oulton Park, on the Isle of Man and in the Hutchinson 100. At the end of 1967, injury interrupted his career yet again, when he sustained a broken arm at Mallory Park, but he worked hard to get fit and finished third in the Ulster Grand Prix.

Hartle was the second man to lap the TT circuit at more than 100 mph, ahead of Surtees. Racing for Hartle was a vocation. He was a gifted and polished rider and although he had twice crashed on the Isle of Man in 1968, he was already planning another season of riding on the Continent when he crashed fatally at Scarborough towards the end of the season.

John Surtees' success made the biggest news, however, and his retirement was to leave Count Agusta with the difficult job of finding a replacement. For British fans particularly, Surtees had become the undoubted grand prix hero, though he was never the most popular of champions. He enjoyed limited rapport with the crowds, did not socialise in the way of, for instance, Hailwood in the 1960s, but he was enormously admired for his supreme professionalism and fine dedication to the sport. There have always been arguments about who was the better rider—Surtees or Geoffrey

Duke—but it is virtually impossible to decide. They reached their peaks at different times and on different machines and, in any event, seldom raced against each other on anything like comparable machinery.

John was born in Surrey in 1934 and received early encouragement from his father, Jack, who had a motor cycle business in Croydon and was also a successful grass track sidecar racer. In the early days John passengered for his father, but his transition to solo riding came on the famous single-cylinder Vincent Grey Flash during his apprenticeship in engineering with the Stevenage firm. He bought himself a 500 cc Manx Norton and as a private entrant on this, and an NSU, was virtually invincible. He showed such talent that he joined the Norton factory team in 1955. That year he won 65 out of the 72 races he rode in. Quiet and modest, Surtees had an exceptional ability as a mechanic and had a rare capacity to sort out an engine. He was 'Man of the Year' in 1958 and '59 in the annual poll run by *Motor Cycle News* and received the MBE for his services to motor cycle racing.

He had been an invaluable acquisition for Count Agusta and when he retired to go car racing, MV were forced to look around once more for someone to uphold their premier status in 500 cc World Championship racing.

Chapter 6

Failing to profit from their racing success

Racing success meant nothing to MV where selling road machines was concerned, for with all their years of grand prix domination, the Italian factory did little to exploit this in the sale of roadsters, especially in export markets. Indeed, except for the export of scooters—notably Vespa and Lambretta—the Italian industry has never made strong export efforts to Britain and if it had not been for the direct approach of British trade interests, few Italian machines would have been available in the United Kingdom.

MV Agusta were as guilty as any of this, but it was rather extraordinary. For when Count Domenico Agusta founded his motor cycle factory in 1946, he started a racing team two years later for the stated purpose of publicising and, more important, proving the products he wanted to sell!

The original aircraft manufacturing concern founded by Count Domenico's father in 1923 was staffed and equipped with the high-level knowledge and equipment required for producing aircraft and, following the ban on aircraft production in Italy immediately after the 1939/45 war, Agusta realised its instant potential for producing lightweight motor cycles—Italy's 'national transport'. Comparative cheapness in both initial cost and running expenses, quite apart from the usually advantageous climate, made small-capacity two-stroke machines extremely popular in post-war Italy and Count Agusta was quick to go into production.

That first 98 cc two-stroke was rapidly followed by a wide range of two- and four-stroke designs which included overhead camshaft versions inspired by the increasing interest in 125 cc racing. Although MV produced a 350 cc twin, the myth of Gallarate for many years was the promise, but never the appearance, of a four-cylinder roadster—for a shaft-driven double overhead camshaft 500 cc four with twin headlights was exhibited at the Milan Show as early as 1951. Yet an actual production version—the weekly *Motor Cycle News* bought the first one as a competition prize—did not appear until the mid-1960s, costing then about £600 ex-works plus tax.

Aware of the growing demand for big capacity machines, MV brought out their four-cylinder roadster as a 600 cc machine, but surprisingly, its ungainly—some even claimed, ugly—appearance inherited very little from the famed 'fire-engine' racers.

Count Agusta's policy clearly followed that of Gilera whose belief was that an extreme, 'unbeatable' racing machine was the best and most convincing publicity for production models. However, where Gilera never considered producing either a racing or a touring version of their 'four', MV's proposed roadster came just three years after the factory began racing with 125 cc singles.

Intriguingly curious now, with two-stroke engine development superior to four-stroke design, is that in 1948/50, 125 cc two-stroke engines were soon eclipsed by single-cylinder, four-stroke double overhead camshaft designs and it was from this development that subsequent multi-cylinder machines were evolved.

However, it was with small engined machines that MV maintained its production to become one of the biggest and most popular in Italy and Spain, where a subsidiary factory was established. But other than this, exports were virtually non-existent except for spasmodic interest by dealers who were interested in racing.

An early success was a 125 cc scooter which had a pressed steel body, swinging arm rear suspension and, unusually, a four-speed gearbox. In the early 1950s, however, the 175 cc overhead cam single was proving itself MV's most popular model, having been exhibited at the Milan Motor Cycle Show in 1952 and '53. Then, in 1954, MV introduced the 125 cc single 'Turismo Rapido', built on similar lines to the 175 cc model.

The first MV road machines to reach Britain were imported in 1956 by the former Brooklands and road-racing ace Ron Harris, of Maidenhead, who established MV Distributors Ltd in Regent Street, London, with racing riders Michael O'Rourke and Derek Minter as his sales representatives both on and off the track.

This venture was by no means a success, for although the riders, O'Rourke particularly, were successful in home racing events, demand for MV road machines was extremely limited and very few were sold. Frankly, at that time, more than 20 years ago, the racy look of small-capacity, lightweight machines was not in keeping with British style or

The 125 cc machine which was displayed at the Milan Show at the end of 1954 (Mick Woollett).

demand and the five model MV range on offer in Britain was far too expensive.

The cheapest model was a 125 cc two-stroke single, the 'Super-Pullman' at £165 including purchase tax. There was also an ohv 125 at £193 and two sporting ohc 175s at £233 and £254. The 'Competizione' ohc 175 cc five-speeder was £434. These figures may seem low by present standards, but when one appreciates that in 1957 a 125 cc BSA Bantam was £94, a 650 cc Triumph Thunderbird cost £245 and a 500 cc Manx Norton was only £481 by comparison, the prices of these MVs were undeniably steep.

Towards the end of the 1950s there was little movement in the MV range in Britain and at the start of 1960 there were just three standard production models available—a 175 cc overhead valve single called the model EL, the 'Tavere'—which was virtually a 250 cc version—and the re-introduced 'Raid', another 250 cc overhead valve model which was new in 1957. A 150 cc scooter came along that year, handled in Britain by Scooter and Continental Imports.

Disregarding the success which he was to enjoy through his British riders—John Surtees, John Hartle, Gary Hocking and Mike Hailwood until 1965—Count Agusta made no attempt to establish a British market and the anticipated demand for the 600 cc four-cylinder roadster did not materialise when the bike eventually appeared in 1965. This was caused by the machine's disappointing styling, sober finish and extreme price.

In the next two years Domenico made strong efforts to give the bike more appeal, lowering the double cradle frame and, in changing the dual seat into a double-decker, making it a more comfortable bike to ride. Detailed changes were apparent in the styling of the headlamp, a new exhaust pipe and silencer arrangement, and an improved shaping for the battery case. The 590 cc engine (56 mm × 60 mm × 4 cylinders) was given more pulling power and developed 52 bhp at 8,000 rpm. The twin 29 mm carburettors were said to give cleaner acceleration and, fitted with an electric starter, 12 volt lighting and MV-four sports Metzeler tyres, the machine's top speed was said to be around 115 mph. In 1967 the machine—full unit construction, shaft drive and five-speed gearbox—was marketed as a 'super luxury touring version of the power-packed 350 and 500 cc racers' and was worth £1,000 in Britain.

Never, however, was anything like the effort applied to MV's racing success evident in the production and marketing of their road machines at an international level. When perhaps a more urgent desire began to show itself, some years later under Count Corrado Agusta, time, progress and competition had overtaken the Italian factory.

Chapter 7

Hocking and Hailwood—four years supreme

With the retirement of Surtees and Ubbiali at the end of 1960 and having won everything there was to win, Count Agusta decided to quit World Championship racing and contest the Italian championships only. This left the Southern Rhodesian rider Gary Hocking stranded. He had only recently been promoted to ride the famous 350 and 500 cc MV fours after his brilliant apprenticeship when he finished second on the lighter MVs in the 125, 250 and 350 cc World Championships of 1960.

He was shaken by Count Agusta's latest move and immediately went after a contract with Honda, who were then making immense efforts in grand prix racing. They did not reply to his request so, when the Count relented and agreed to provide him with 350 and 500 cc machines for the World Championships, together with a couple of mechanics, Hocking jumped at the chance.

Possibly in an effort to counter some of the criticism which MV had attracted, somewhat unfairly, through their succession of so-called 'cheap' victories after all their main competitors had retired, the Count wanted to make it clear that Hocking's bikes should not be full-blown works entries. An 'MV Privat' badge was stuck on the fuel tanks, but the masquerade fooled few people in the know, particularly as the season wore on and MV works mechanics could be seen looking after the machines. At the time the Count was pre-occupied with the Italian motor cycle market which had slumped. The FIMs decision to increase the number of classic races from five to seven in the 350 cc class and from seven to ten in the 500 cc class, with all the additional work, organisation and investment which that would entail, also had an influence on his decision to pull out from direct competition. He withdrew MV from the lighter classes altogether so that in 1961, for the first time since 1949 in the 125 cc class and since 1955 in the

The front row of the grid at the Dutch TT in 1961. Gary Hocking (1) on the MV with the Nortons of Mike Hailwood (2) and Frank Perris (24) alongside. Hocking won from Hailwood and Bob McIntyre (Mick Woollett).

Hocking on the MV leads McIntyre in the 350 cc event of the Dutch TT in 1961 to score an impressive double victory (Mick Woollett).

250 cc class, there were no official entries from MV. It remains an interesting speculation for many racing buffs to ponder whether Honda, who came into racing with impact for the first time in 1960, would have been able to take the 125 cc world titles in 1961 with such ease, or even at all, had the MVs still been running. It aroused as many arguments as did the speculation about MV's own success in the heavier classes after Gilera and Guzzi had withdrawn at the end of 1957!

Gary Hocking, however, proved a worthy successor to John Surtees in MV's growing list of star riders, although he stayed with the Italian factory only about 18 months, until the middle of 1962. Hocking had followed the example of fellow countrymen Ray Amm and Jim Redman in setting out for Britain in search of fame and fortune on the motor cycle racing circuits of Europe. He entered his first TT in 1959 when he finished 12th on a Norton in the Junior event. In his first year with MV he rode to those highly commendable second places in the three lower capacity classes. But after Count Agusta had seriously recruited Mike Hailwood, Hocking was never altogether happy. He saw

Hailwood's presence as a threat to his own position with MV. His relationship with Count Agusta became strained and his battles with Hailwood in 1961 and '62 were momentous, especially their great duel in the 350 cc TT of 1962. Hocking left motor cycle racing prematurely at the TTs that year. By this time he was disillusioned with MV and particularly became so upset by the death of his good friend Tom Phillis in the Junior TT, while the latter was desperately trying to push the less powerful Honda ahead of the faster MVs of Hailwood and Hocking himself, that after winning the Senior race he left the island and went home to Southern Rhodesia. He said he was finished with racing after seeing the sport he loved claim the lives of his two friends Ray Amm and then Tom Phillis. The personal disaster for Gary was that, on being tempted into car racing later that same year, he was killed during a Formula 1 race at the Natal Grand Prix.

However, in 1961 Hocking rode the MVs very well, taking the 350 machine to wins in Holland, East Germany, Northern Ireland and Italy. On the 500 MV his record was excellent. He won in West

On the way to the 350 cc world title—Gary Hocking takes the 350 cc MV four to victory in the Ulster Grand Prix (B.R. Nicholls).

Germany, France, Holland, Belgium, East Germany, Northern Ireland and Sweden, winning the title by a margin of eight points from Hailwood who, during the latter part of the season, had been riding MV machinery.

Standing out from the season were the 350 cc race of the Dutch TT when Hocking's controversial tactics brought him a telling off from Count Agusta, and his two-race battle with Hailwood in the Italian Grand Prix at Monza. In Holland Hocking was determined to win, having been beaten into second place by Phil Read on a Norton in the Isle of Man. A duel developed between Gary on the MV and Bob McIntyre riding a Bianchi. With only half a lap to go McIntyre was in the lead, but Hocking thrust the MV in pursuit and on the final lap, in an enormous effort to take the lead, leaned on the Scottish rider and thundered his way through the narrow gap to take the lead and win the race. It was claimed that Gary afterwards apologised to McIntyre, but Count Agusta was not pleased.

For MV fans gathered on the Isle of Man, however, 1961 was a year of total disaster. They won not one race. The 250 MV could not live with the Honda 250 fours, the 350 cc machine went off song at the crucial time and in the Senior event Hailwood on a Manx Norton was untouchable.

Monza in 1961 brought the first major clash between Hocking and Hailwood on MVs. The two riders had duelled before, as early as 1959 when Hailwood was riding a Ducati and Hocking an MZ. When Count Agusta offered Hailwood rides at Monza it was a blow to Hocking and he was determined to show the MV boss that he could beat Hailwood. He overcame Hailwood's challenge in the 350 cc event, but in the 500 cc clash the two were having a tremendous scrap when Hocking crashed after his footrest had dug into the ground, leaving Hailwood to race ahead to win.

The two riders had earlier been friendly enough, but Hocking resented Hailwood's intrusion into MV's fortunes. Yet in a way it was not surprising that Mike should be tempted by the Italian factory's interest. In the very early days when Mike was working unhappily at Triumph he successfully pestered his father, Stan, to allow him to race and made his debut at an Easter Monday meeting at Oulton Park on a single-cylinder MV. Racing machines from MV had started coming into Britain in the early 1950s and by 1955 Ron Harris, a former Brooklands racer, was spending his time trying to sell the Italian machines in the UK. As already noted he employed Derek Minter and Michael O'Rourke as salesmen during the week and they went round trying to interest dealers in the MVs. Indeed, it was on the MVs that Derek Minter made his Oulton Park debut. But in 1957 it was the two MVs belonging to Bill Webster that attracted Hailwood Senior. Count Agusta had let Bill have the bikes on condition that they be raced by top riders only, since he did not want to risk MV's already formidable reputation with a spate of poor results or breakdowns by inexperienced riders. But Stan Hailwood was Bill's friend and he was very persuasive. Eventually the well-known Crewe dealer agreed to lend Mike the single-knocker machine and, together, Stan and Bill set to work to put it in racing fettle. Bill was entered on the double-knocker MV in the same race and was able to see Mike Hailwood's racing potential at close quarters. He later told Stan privately that he was sure his son was World Champion material.

It was through Bill Webster again that Mike was offered MV rides in 1961. Bill, who by this time had built a reputation as a talent scout for Count Agusta, had told Domenico all about Hailwood's ability. The Count saw Mike in action on the MVs at Monza, when Mike won the 500 cc race and came second to Hocking in the 350 cc event, and agreed with Bill Webster that he should be riding MVs on a regular basis. Mike was keen to move up into the heavier classes and with no other works bikes available there was a queue of riders trying to get their hands on the MVs. The Count, claimed Hailwood, simply *told* him to join the team and that was that. There was no opportunity for him to say no even if he had wanted!

So for 1962 Hailwood joined Hocking on the MVs and prepared to face a strong challenge from Honda in the 350 cc class, the Japanese factory competing for the first time on new, modified versions of their successful 250 cc four-cylinder racer. It was now clear that there would be little cooperation between the two MV riders and, in spite of what instructions Count Agusta might have

MVs together. Mike Hailwood (3) manages to overtake Hocking at Ramsey hairpin on his way to victory in the Junior TT of 1962 (Mick Woollett).

issued, Hailwood and Hocking would each be riding to win. The Junior TT proved an outstanding battle and the two MVs raced almost as one throughout the 226½ miles, Hailwood finally winning by seven seconds at an average speed of 99.59 mph.

It was a remarkable duel. Hailwood was flagged away ten seconds ahead of Hocking and for most of the time they raced within ten feet of each other. They even came into the pits together with the crowds really on their toes. Then, on the fifth lap, Mike made his move and had gained five seconds at the Grandstand, eight at Ramsey. Hocking responded and rode so well that the gap was cut down to five seconds. At about this point both MVs began misfiring, but Hailwood retained the initiative and won an outstanding race with a new lap record of 101.58 mph.

In the Senior race that year another epic was on the cards as Hocking started first and Hailwood 30 seconds later. Tension and excitement rose as Mike was only one second in arrears on corrected times after the first lap, but the battle never developed. The MV had clutch trouble and Hocking raced on to win comfortably, establishing a new lap record at 105.75 mph. The tragic accident to Tom Phillis ended Hocking's motor cycle racing career and terminated what might have been a tremendous season-long inter-MV battle. After Hocking had gone, Hailwood was left to fight MV's battle single-handed. Against the now quite old 350 MV, scaled down versions of the famous 500s, the new Hondas had the edge and Jim Redman was too good a rider to throw away the advantage. He beat Hailwood into second place in Holland and East Germany and won four of the six grands prix to take the 350 cc crown. It was the first time in four years that MV had not won the 350 cc World Championship and if Count Agusta took the defeat to heart he could find consolation in Hailwood's performance in the 500 cc class. With little real opposition the powerful four-cylinder MV won the first six grands prix and Hailwood himself achieved five outright wins.

Until Hailwood mounted the MV at Monza at the end of 1961, all his successes had been scored on single-cylinder machines and it says much for his abundant talent that he rode the MV four to instant success. Mike had an impressive pedigree when he joined MV, becoming 250 cc World Champion on a Honda in 1961 and before that gaining repeated successes on British circuits. In 1958, when only 18, he won three out of four A-CU Road Racing Stars and did even better the following year by winning all four solo Road Racing Stars, a feat he repeated in 1960. With his first 500 cc world title on the MV in

1962 and a runner-up place in the 350 cc category for the same factory, Hailwood was now on the threshold of a massive run of success riding Count Agusta's machines. For the next three years MV, with Hailwood, continued to dominate the 500 cc championship series.

The record was exceptional, even by MV standards. In the four years 1962–65, Hailwood took the MV to an astronomical 27 classic wins in the 500 cc class, breaking a vast number of race and lap records. On occasions when Hailwood's name did not appear in the results it was because he had not competed, the championship having already been won. Alternatively he missed out because of injury. Although in these years the 350 MV was no match for the powerful Honda of Jim Redman, Hailwood was second in 1962 and 1963 and third in 1965. In 1963 the MV was only four points behind Redman's Honda.

In 1963 MV won the premier championship in spite of an enterprising move by former World Champion Geoffrey Duke which brought the 1957 Gileras out of mothballs, but in the end the much-anticipated pitched battle between the two Italian marques never fully materialised. With this challenge over, MV swept through the 500 cc rounds in 1964 with Hailwood putting on a dazzling display of six wins in six races. At Daytona for the American Grand Prix, Hailwood took the reliable MV to a new One Hour Record, before going on to win the World Championship race in the afternoon. Wins in the Senior TT and in Holland, Belgium, West and East Germany followed to give MV the championship by 15 points from Jack Ahearn on a Norton. Although Hailwood had strong rider opposition in some races from people like Phil Read, John Hartle and Derek Minter, the MV was far superior to the Nortons and Matchlesses which opposed it.

An interesting prospective challenge at the beginning of the season came from one of the few South American riders ever to make an impact on international racing, Benedicto Caldarella. The Argentinian had got hold of one of the Gilera fours used the previous year in the Geoff Duke challenge and on this classic machine he threw down the gauntlet to MV and Hailwood. In the opening round at Daytona he set hearts pounding by running the MV uncomfortably close. For 14 long laps of the American Speedbowl he stayed close to Hailwood, always threatening, but then gearbox trouble on the Gilera ended the challenge.

In Holland, in June, Caldarella once again gave the MV a hard ride and the Argentinian stuck close to Mike. Sweeping through the long curve which leads to the grandstand straight, the two were almost as one, but then Caldarella lost control and the Gilera careered on to the grass and collided with the straw bales. Although he did well to regain the track and continue the pursuit, the MV was taken on to win.

This has been one of the features of MV's success over the years. It might not always have been the fastest machine in the race, but it tended to be more reliable than many which challenged it and was, at its best, sometimes easier to ride. Of course, it had so much power compared with the single-cylinder Nortons and Matchlesses and, on the more open circuits like Francorchamps in Belgium, this could be put to good use. The rider's talent was tested much more, however, on Britain's short circuits like Brands Hatch and Mallory Park and the crowds turned out in thousands to see Hailwood keep the heavy four-cylinder machines under control. In six years of racing up to 1962 Hailwood estimated that he had ridden at least 14 different makes of machine from a 50 cc two-stroke to the 500 cc four-cylinder MV and including two-strokes, poppet and desmodromic valved four-strokes, and single, twin and four-cylinder engines. He said the big MV four was the one he enjoyed riding most, partly because it presented such a challenge. 'The MV develops so much power that I am not at all sure that anyone has yet succeeded in getting the best out of it, simply because the rider's limitations are greater than those of the bike', he once said.

By 1965 MV had enjoyed things going their way in the 500 cc class for seven consecutive seasons and had collected the manufacturers world title in the same category for the same number of years. But the monopoly which they similarly held in the 350 cc class for four years from 1958 had been relinquished to Honda who, through that great rider and tactician Jim Redman, had dominated this championship. Count Agusta felt that this class too should rightly be MV's and it needled him to see Honda so strong. For 1965 MV brought out a new machine and a new rider. The brand new three-cylinder was intended to replace the massive four and was lighter, had a smaller frontal area and handled better: in the hands of their own riding prodigy, by name Giacomo Agostini, it all but took the title from Honda.

Honda's strength was still Jim Redman, while Yamaha mounted a strong challenge through Phil Read, who had taken the 250 cc title for Yamaha the previous season, but in the opening rounds at the Nürburgring all honours went to MV with Agostini and Hailwood riding home first and second. It was something of a shock win for the young, handsome

Italian rider, but Count Agusta was confident that the new machines were capable of taking the 350 cc crown as Agostini prepared for his Isle of Man debut. He made a visit to the island more than two weeks before the races and spent time learning the circuit on a Royal Enfield roadster. At this time Hailwood was still MV's premier rider, but although Mike won the Senior race it was Agostini who made the listings in the Junior event, though he had to be content with third place behind Redman and Read. Redman was not going to surrender the title easily. He won the next three rounds in Holland, East Germany and Czechoslovakia and the battle seemed almost to be over as MV struggled, with only the Dutch TT bringing any kind of result, Hailwood and Agostini finishing second and third. But after winning in Finland and then Italy, before his home crowd, Agostini brought MV right back into the picture. A win in the final round in Japan could secure the title for MV and before their home crowd, it turned out the Honda was very nearly humiliated. The handsome Italian was holding a commanding lead until the MV suffered a broken contact-breaker spring. He finished fifth, but it was MV's day, for Hailwood raced on to win, with Redman doing enough in second place to retain the title by just eight points.

MV could look back on a good season, with a first and second in the 500 cc championship and a second and third in the 350 cc class, but Hailwood was already becoming restless. He was contemplating a move to four-wheel racing and during the year had competed in a number of Formula 1 events. Because of the lack of real opposition to the big 500 MV, he was not enjoying the same excitement in winning one grand prix after another in tedious succession. It was also obvious that Agostini was to be groomed for stardom by Count Agusta and Hailwood's relationship with the Count had at times been turbulent to say the least, mainly through the latter's frequent unpredict-ability and the way in which he sometimes withheld permission for Mike to ride at British meetings. When Honda's eyes focused on the 500 cc World Championship and looked in Hailwood's direction as the obvious rider to bring them their one remaining ambition in world motor cycle racing, it was not surprising that he, after being offered what was reported to be the most lucrative contract ever in motor cycle racing, should decide to switch camps.

Stanley Michael Bailey Hailwood was born in Oxford in 1940 and made his racing debut on a 125 cc MV in 1957. That winter he went to South Africa to gain racing experience and came back with a pocketful of trophies. On his return he quickly made an impact on British racing and in 1958, when only 18, was 3rd, 7th, 12th and 13th in the four solo classes on the Isle of Man. In 1960 he became the second man to lap the Mountain Course at over 100 mph on a single-cylinder machine. His first classic win was the Ulster Grand Prix of 1959 on a Ducati. That year he reached third place in the 125 cc World Championship. Although he made enormous impact in Britain and elsewhere on other machines —his first world title was won on a privately-entered 250 cc Honda in 1961—it is fair to say that his career with MV brought him the greatest recognition, when he won the most coveted 500 cc world title on the Italian machines from 1962 to 1965. The pinnacle of his career coincided with Britain's 'swinging Sixties' when for the first time in road racing history, riders like Bill Ivy, Phil Read, Giacomo Agostini and, most of all perhaps, Mike Hailwood himself, became new cult figures admired by thousands all over Europe and beyond. The 1960s were also MV's most exciting, dynamic and successful period as a racing factory, certainly in the 500 cc class. The decade witnessed the Hocking-Hailwood and the Hailwood-Agostini battles, there was Geoffrey Duke's courageous and enterprising move in persuading Gilera to loan him their fabulous 1957 machines to throw down the gauntlet to MV, Hailwood had his astonishing record-breaking day on the MV at Daytona, and behind it all Count Domenico Agusta, the driving force behind everything MV did in those days, was still alive. The 1960s will also be long remembered for the two-season fight for the 500 cc world crown between reigning champions MV and the challengers from Japan, Honda.

Like most MV non-Italian team riders, Mike Hailwood often found Count Agusta hard to get along with, though, like all of them except perhaps Les Graham, he never had the chance to get to know him really well. Mike used to get annoyed at being kept waiting, occasionally for an hour or two, after he had flown out to Italy specially to see the Count. Mind you, Mike was never the most patient of people. He complained that the Count was inflexible and that once he gave an order there was no arguing against his decision. At times he would be charming, at other times infuriating, but although Mike did not always see eye-to-eye with his Italian boss (indeed, he had the mother-and-father of all rows after he had ridden at Imola against the Gileras of Hartle and Minter when Count Agusta thought that for the good name of MV he should not have done), it was not entirely the 'difficult' personality of Count Agusta which

precipitated his move to Honda. As we have seen, there were a number of reasons, not the least being that Mike was anxious to do more riding. MV were not interested in the 250 cc class, but with Honda he had the chance of racing in this highly competitive category, plus the 350 and 500 cc classes in which MV competed.

Hailwood had a number of brilliant and outstanding rides on the MV and he once said that if he had the choice he would always ride the big MV 500 in the TTs, for he felt it was perfect for the job. It is perhaps not surprising therefore that the demanding Mountain Course became the background to some of his most historic rides on MV bikes. In 1964, for instance, Hailwood rode to victory in the Senior TT while still suffering from the effects of flu and after being strongly advised by the RAC doctor not to ride. In 1965, when Hailwood and MV were seen together for the last time on the island, the combination produced memorable performances. In the Junior race the new three-cylinder machine which the factory had produced for Hailwood, proved troublesome. Virtually untried, it had capitulated during practice at the West German Grand Prix in the opening round of the season, when Hailwood had been forced to take the old four-cylinder machine for the race to finish second to Agostini, who took the MV three to its first major win.

In the Isle of Man the machine was handling so badly that Mike was only able to complete two laps of practice. The works mechanics worked through the night cannibalising the old 500 of forks and shock absorbers, but there was little time to test out the 'new' machine on race morning. World Champion Jim Redman was expected to win the race and the predictions looked like coming true as he set off at a good pace. The MV was flagged away some 30 seconds later, but after a sluggish start, news soon filtered through that Hailwood was gaining on Redman. On the first lap Hailwood bettered his own record from a standing start and cut 20 seconds into Redman's time advantage actually to lead the race. It did not last and on the second lap the MV began to falter and on lap three Hailwood had to pull into the pits with the chain overstretched by four inches. The back wheel was covered in oil and although the mechanics tightened as many nuts as they could find, the oil continued to escape. Mike set off again but had to admit defeat after only another 13 miles. Stan Hailwood said at the time that if Count Agusta had allowed Mike to ride the new machine at Monza the previous September, where there was nothing at stake, the shortcomings of that type of chain would have been seen. 'And with a good bike I think the 350 cc race record would have stood for a long time', said Stan.

The Senior TT that same year was also unforgettable. The MVs of Hailwood and Agostini were expected to dominate, but in the wet Agostini fell at Sarah's Cottage but was unhurt. Comfortably in the lead at the end of the third lap, Hailwood looked a certain winner. Then, at Sarah's Cottage again, the powerful MV struck a small deposit of oil and at 80 mph the machine hurtled out of control as Hailwood came off. Shaken, but substantially unhurt, Mike surveyed the battered MV. It was in a sorry state, with the fairing badly scarred, megaphones flattened and the windscreen cracked. Half a footrest had been severed, the gear lever was twisted out of true and the handlebars were badly bent. He hauled the bike upright and propped it against the bank. He kicked the handlebars into some sort of acceptable shape and then, strictly against the regulations, pushed the bike downhill and against the direction of the race until it fired.

The machine looked a wreck as Hailwood brought the MV into the pits, its windscreen flapping dangerously. While Mike remained mounted the mechanics did what they could, including ripping off the remnants of the windscreen. Mike set off once more and at 160 mph, his face exposed to the wind and the cutting rain, had now to contend with a throttle that insisted on sticking open. He pulled the MV into the pits once more and was expected then to retire. Instead he re-joined the race, urging the MV forward once again. The throttle-slide still would not close down and Hailwood's only option was to control the power of the MV on the corners by using his hand brake. He won the race at an average speed of 91.69 mph, the slowest Senior win on the island for some 15 years. But it was one of the most glorious wins and one of the most memorable races of Hailwood's long and distinguished two-wheel racing career, and continued to be talked about long after Hailwood and MV parted company.

Chapter 8

The Gilera confrontation

When Mike Hailwood rode the big MV to its fifth outright win of the season at Monza towards the end of 1962, he clinched the 500 cc World Championship for MV for the fifth season running. Even for the Italian factory's most passionate fans, the predictable nature of their continued success was beginning to wear just a little thin. For many others, the 500 cc championships were already a big yawn.

One man who felt driven to do something about it was former World Champion Geoffrey Duke. Duke had reluctantly left Norton in 1953 to ride for Gilera when it was clear that the racing days of the British factory were at an end. Similarly, once Gilera had put up the racing shutters in 1957, he soldiered on for a couple of seasons but then, again with no competitive machinery available on which to tackle the MV, he retired.

Duke had a great deal of respect for the Gilera racers and he did not relish the unchallenged success of his former rival, MV. The Gileras he and his team mate Reg Armstrong had ridden in 1957 were outstanding multi-cylinder machines which, in spite of their sometimes doubtful handling characteristics, were certainly among the best in the world. Lack of competition meant that the 1963

Out come the 1957 Gileras to challenge the record-breaking MVs. Geoff Duke is seen with John Hartle and Derek Minter (on the bike) during tests at Monza (Mick Woollett).

MVs had not seen all that much development work in the intervening years. Could the six-year-old Gileras still be a match for the current MVs?

Duke could not get the prospect of Gilera and MV fighting it out once more in the classic series out of his mind. The old machines were still under wraps in the famous Arcore factory, but if he could obtain their loan from Gilera he could form his own small team and try to knock MV off their perch. But he first had to persuade the Gilera bosses to let him have the bikes and that was not easy.

In fact the idea had taken root some time before, in 1960 or '61 and had been discussed jointly as a proposition between Duke, Reg Armstrong and Bob McIntyre—all former Gilera riders. But when the idea was taken to Gilera they were not really interested. Duke persisted, but it took a long time for Gilera to give their agreement and then it was only on condition that Bob McIntyre rode the bikes. Bob had earned enormous respect from old man Gilera after winning the One Hour Record for him in 1957 with a 350 cc machine—a remarkable achievement which Gilera had personally witnessed; but by the time Duke got permission to go ahead, Bob was riding under contract to Honda and was not able to accept Geoff's invitation to ride the Gileras: he crashed fatally in 1962 before the scheme got off the ground. The old rivalry which existed between the two famous Italian factories put a sharp edge on Duke's proposition. It was bright, novel, adventurous and the move would be sure to capture the motor cycling public's imagination. Gilera would be in the spotlight once more and that might help domestic sales at hardly any cost to themselves. What is more, if MV had become complacent through lack of competition, Gilera might just pinch the world title from them.

Duke persisted and with Gilera's final agreement, Derek Minter now became the key figure in the drama. First, Gilera wanted to be sure that the old machines would not disgrace his illustrious company's name. The factory agreed that Duke should have the machines tested and, if they showed themselves still to be competitive, they would loan Duke the bikes.

It was an historic moment when the old bikes were wheeled out for high speed testing at the famous Monza circuit. Duke's riding days were over, of course, but he recruited the very talented Derek Minter—an exceptionally gifted rider then at the peak of his career—and John Hartle to put the Gileras through their paces. They certainly made those bikes fly. Both riders were soon lapping consistently at around 116 mph. Minter rode magnificently, hurtling round at more than 118

mph to come within a fraction of MV's own lap record set up by John Surtees. It was the fastest any Gilera had been raced round the Monza circuit. They were satisfied, the plan was given the green light, and the 1963 season bristled with expectancy at the prospect of a serious challenge to the MV for the first time in six years.

The whole thing was an entirely private venture with Geoffrey Duke financing the deal, with the promise of help, it was said, from Castrol, but Gilera put nothing into the scheme except the release of the bikes. Minter and Hartle were confirmed as the Gilera riders to race under the 'Scuderia Duke' banner and the battle was on. First sight of the Gileras was at Silverstone in the Hutchinson 500 meeting. The weather was diabolical, but the fans turned out in force to see the Italian machines in action once more and they were not disappointed. In a good curtain raiser to the season, Minter and Hartle crossed the line first and second.

At Brands Hatch the Gilera come-back continued to bite deeply. Derek was the uncrowned King of Brands and had become a traditional favourite there after John Surtees had deserted home circuits to follow the grand prix trail. Underlying the MV-Gilera battle was a more personal confrontation. Minter and Hailwood were old foes from their British short circuit days and, while Hailwood had gone on to conquer the grand prix circuits, Minter had remained faithful to home fans and had become probably the best short circuit racer in the land with a superb style and a dashing habit of starting badly and storming his way excitingly through the field to finish at the front.

At Brands he was virtually unbeatable, and once again it was Gilera's big day. The disappointment was that the Gilera-MV clash did not materialise because Hailwood crashed in the opening 350 cc race while riding an AJS and withdrew from the remainder of the programme, including the 500 cc race in which he would have been up against the Gileras. Through Minter the Gilera won the 500 and 1,000 cc races. John Hartle finished second in the latter. Hailwood, meantime, was cut and bruised following his fall and later had it confirmed that he had chipped a bone in his left hand. In winning the 1,000 cc event, Minter took the Gilera round at 90.34 mph to become the first rider to lap the Kent circuit at more than 90 mph.

Excitement mounted in these early season non-championship meetings leading up to the opening grand prix rounds as the Gileras were raced at Oulton Park and, before 50,000 spectators, bettered the previous lap record twice, first through

Hailwood on the MV did not only have the Gileras to contend with in 1963. Here he is seen (1) being led by Gyula Marsovszky on a 496 cc Matchless at Mallory Park (B.R. Nicholls).

Minter and then Hartle. Then, at Imola, with Hailwood riding the MV while still suffering the effects of his injured wrist, the Gileras once again showed the MVs the way home. Hailwood and Silvio Grassetti, on the other MV, moved off fastest with Minter and Hartle in hot pursuit after a poor start. After five laps Hailwood's bike was still in front, but five laps later Minter was resting the Gilera on the MV's rear wheel and on lap 12, at about the half-way stage, he was able to flash ahead. The MVs were beaten while Gilera collected an exciting one-two.

Those who at first had rather dismissed the Gilera come-back as a trivial novelty were now taking notice: not least the MV factory and Mike Hailwood. If the Gileras could match this kind of performance in the World Championship rounds, then MV were in for their toughest battle in years.

Behind the scenes, however, there were minor irritations in the Gilera camp. At Imola, Minter later claimed, Hartle was able to out-accelerate him consistently coming out of a curve and he could not understand the reason. 'The only way I could beat him was to out-brake him into the corners', said Derek, 'and it wasn't until later that I realised that Hartle, although he was supposed to be my supporting rider, had been given the best engine.'

Much later in the season Minter had another disagreement with Duke, but what might now be seen as the crucial day in the Gilera challenge to MV came, not when the two machines were battling on the track, but at a domestic meeting at Brands Hatch. It was in May, before the grand prix season had got into its stride. In one of the most exciting races seen at Brands Hatch, Derek Minter was hurtling towards yet another almost certain success. At Dingle Dell, on the final lap, Dave Downer, in a desperate effort to move ahead of Minter, rode into the rear of Derek's machine and in the crash that followed Downer was killed and Minter broke his back.

It was a bitter setback to the Gilera effort. While Minter recovered, Phil Read was drafted into the team and in the opening round of the World Championships, on the Isle of Man, the Gileras finished second and third with Hailwood managing to keep the MV ahead. Hartle rode a magnificent race, averaging over 103 mph with a fastest lap of more than 105 mph. But MV and Hailwood were still untouchable, giving a remarkable performance. They set a record for the race at 104.64 mph and also a new lap record at 106.64 mph. Hailwood had realised before the race that he had to carry the MV fight to Gilera. Those early season wins had given the Gilera team a great deal of confidence and although Minter's injury had been unfortunate, there was still a lot of optimism in the Gilera camp. Hailwood knew he had somehow to demoralise the Gilera team. Winning simply was not enough. He set out as a matter of deliberate policy to ride every 500 cc lap, both in practice and the race itself, at more than 100 mph. It was a remarkable feat which set the island buzzing and did a lot for MV's flagging morale.

However, in Holland, in the second round of the championship, Gilera took advantage when Hailwood dropped out, and finished first and second, Hartle, in Minter's continued absence, assuming the senior role. With Hailwood taking the MV to victory in Belgium, the championship was still well contested as the riders prepared for the Ulster Grand Prix. Minter had made a remarkable recovery from his injury and had already chalked up record-breaking speeds in tests on the Monza circuit and at Oulton Park. He was pronounced fit for the gruelling Irish race, but a niggling disagreement with Geoffrey Duke at Liverpool involving travel arrangements to Belfast did not get the expedition off to the best of starts.

The bumpy Irish circuit played havoc with Minter's back and he seemed to have trouble steering the big Gilera. Meantime, on the more reliable MV, Hailwood had a good ride to finish in front, with Hartle's and Minter's Gileras in second and third positions. The MV had now won three of the four grands prix, to Gilera's sole victory in

Holland, so the race in East Germany at Sachsenring was vital to Gilera's challenge. Hartle was the better placed Gilera rider and if he could outrace Hailwood in East Germany Mike would be forced to continue the fight to keep his crown. But John had a bad race and, as he crashed, a mudguard came off the Gilera and just missed Minter's head. Hailwood, meantime, pushed on to take the race. It seemed certain now that MV had successfully held off the Gilera challenge and the outcome was put beyond doubt as Hailwood went on to win in the three remaining rounds, in Finland, Italy and the Argentine.

To be fair, Gilera in the latter stages were unlucky. For the Finnish Grand Prix there was only one machine available. Read had crashed one in the Ulster and Hartle's prang in East Germany had put another out of action.

The Gileras had made Hailwood fight harder than usual for his 500 cc world title and Stan Hailwood said that Mike had realised when he fell off at Brands Hatch early in the year, that retaining the title would be no joy ride. Said Stan: 'It was then that Mike realised that racing was a serious business'.

Derek Minter said later that the Gileras were still very quick bikes when they were brought out in 1963, but they were difficult to steer. The MV, in comparison with the Honda 500, which was yet to come for Hailwood, was docile, handled superbly and he was later to say that it was the finest all-round machine he had ever ridden.

In the opinion of noted motor cycling journalist Charlie Rous, however, who stayed close to all the action during those days of 1963, it was Minter's crash at Brands that ruined Duke's lively scheme. Said Charlie: 'If that hadn't happened I think Derek would have been World Champion in 1963 and MV's long run of success in 500 cc racing would have been interrupted'.

Chapter 9

Record breaking at Daytona

The 500 cc World Championship had an additional round in 1964 at Daytona in the United States and this 'glamour' round at the sweeping Florida Speedbowl opened the season. Hailwood was up for his third 500 cc world title in three years and a win at Daytona would put MV on the championship trail once more.

The racing machinery was little advanced from the previous season and in the 500 cc class the opposition had got no keener. The MV was expected to win, although the South American Benedicto Caldarella was likely to run Hailwood close, riding a Gilera four obtained through his family, who worked for Gilera in South America. With Hailwood at Daytona were his father, Stan, and British speed record expert Charlie Rous, at that time on the editorial staff of *Motor Cycle News*. Before leaving for America, Rous had mentioned to Stan and Mike that Daytona would be an ideal opportunity to attack the world One Hour Record, which had been set at 143 mph by Bob McIntyre on a Gilera 350 cc four at Monza as long ago as 1957. Since then the Monza circuit had deteriorated to the extent that it was not fit for the Hour record attempt—indeed it had been far from ideal when McIntyre took the record seven years before.

Mike was keen to have a go and knew he had a good chance on the MV, because the year before at Daytona he had lapped the famous circuit at 139.06 mph on his personal Norton. He reckoned the MV was worth an extra 10 mph.

The problem was Count Agusta. He vetoed the idea. Stan Hailwood cabled him from Daytona asking for a go-ahead decision, but the Count turned him down. For a start he was more concerned to win the United States Grand Prix and did not want to prejudice that success through any side-tracks into world record attempts, however tempting. The other problem was the almost total lack of special preparation. The MV contingent had only two machines at Daytona, the grand prix race-prepared machine and a practice bike. They did not have too many spares either, so if anything went seriously wrong they could have been in real trouble. It seemed like the end of a good if risky idea as the MV team, reluctantly, packed the practice

bike back into its crate ready for shipping back to Europe.

Even more dejected were the Daytona authorities. It would have been a tremendous boost for their circuit for a new One Hour Record to be attempted there and they wanted the idea to go through. According to Stan Hailwood's account of the affair, they sent an urgent cable to the Count in Italy asking him to change his mind. Said Stan: 'The reply came back to me and to my amazement the Count said yes'.

According to other sources, it seems anything but certain that Count Agusta ever did give his clearance for the attempt to take place. Asked about it recently, Charlie Rous said: 'Stan Hailwood is dead now, but he simply told Vittorio Carruana (the Italian mechanic) that he had cabled the Count and it was okay to go ahead. But I think it's doubtful if permission was given. Stan came to me and said "Let's get on with it" '.

All the necessary officials like timekeepers and observers from the FIM were at the circuit for the grand prix and in the end the temptation to let Mike have a go at the record just proved too much. Stan made up his mind to go ahead on the eve of the grand prix, so there was no time for realistic preparation. The attempt would have to be made on the morning of the World Championship race (which was to take place in the afternoon) with the practice machine.

As dawn broke over Daytona, Hailwood Senior started things moving. He woke Charlie Rous and the two of them then got Vittorio out of bed. While Rous and the Italian mechanic went to get the bike ready, Stan Hailwood let Mike sleep for a while. The tyres were changed, the fairing refitted and a high gear sprocket put on, but the machine was really not equipped for such an attempt. At about 9.00 am the bike was as ready as it could be and Stan telephoned Mike and told him the attack on the record was on and to get to the track immediately. Meantime, Charlie Rous went to fetch the essential timekeepers. The desire of the circuit organisers to see the attempt go ahead did not prevent them from charging Stan Hailwood for the use of the track. Explained Charlie Rous: 'He wanted it, effectively, for little more than an hour and there was nothing going on there that morning. All the same, they charged him for the use of the track. There were other expenses and also certain fees charged by the FIM. At about three dollars to the pound in those days, I reckon that the entire attempt must have cost Stan Hailwood the best part of £1,000'.

Stan was not short of cash, however, and it would have been money he was happy to spend, if Mike was to take the record. The attempt was master-minded by Charlie Rous, who had specialised in record breaking attempts and was one of only about three or four European reporters present. Explained Charlie recently: 'There was nothing inferior about the bike which Mike used. It just happened to be the spare but, of course, was not as good as the grand prix racer. It did its 10,000 rpm and all that, but in fact it had a Dunlop front tyre and an Avon back tyre. This, for the simple reason we didn't have sufficient tyres. It was a straightforward road racing machine, with a road racing fairing. It was fuelled with petrol, not alcohol, and it was geared for 10,000 rpm. Vittorio put it on a high gear'.

Charlie remembers that it was a beautiful morning. The fuel tank was filled to its 45 litres capacity. Major David Goode, of the FIM, then insisted that Hailwood should circulate no nearer the inside edge of the track than a ten feet line, which was in fact marked. This was used as a measurement line so that it was possible to be positive about the distance covered. The local meteorological office forecast fine and rather cool weather and with Charlie Rous detailed to do the MV camp's timekeeping and Hailwood Senior in charge of the signalling, everything seemed ready.

Said Stan Hailwood shortly afterwards: 'Tyres were a problem so I decided to keep a special watch on them and borrowed a pair of powerful binoculars for the purpose'.

The MV sounded in good shape as Mike waited for the start. It was a standing start with the engine running. Then Major Goode dropped the Union Jack and the record attempt was on. The MV's first lap was taken at 136.5 mph, much below the required speed to take the record, and it was then

Charlie Rous checks the tyre pressures of the MV at Daytona, watched by Stan Hailwood in the cowboy hat, prior to the new One Hour Record in 1964 (B.R. Nicholls).

that Stan Hailwood realised he had made a miscalculation. He had overlooked the standing start. He had set a target of 145 mph and the first lap timing fell well short. 'I began to wonder how many laps it would take to pull up to the required 145 mph', said Stan at the time.

After 15 minutes, with Mike lapping at more than 146 mph, the average was up to 141 mph and after half an hour of riding the MV was still averaging only 142.9 mph. Stan decided to hang out the 'hurry up' signs and Mike hoisted the average to 145.2 mph after 45 minutes. In Charlie Rous' words, there was no attempt to go for a colossal record. It was simply that McIntyre's record on the Gilera had stood for seven years and was there for the taking. Surprisingly, nobody had attempted it at all. Rous said: 'Ontario wasn't built then, Monza was in too bad a state, so Daytona was the only place for a new record to be made, since then it was only four or five years old, perfectly smooth, banked and basically a much faster circuit than Monza'.

Towards the end the MV slowed and observers saw Mike look back towards the rear wheel. Hailwood Senior immediately thought of tyre problems, but could see no tell-tale white signs. As the MV thundered past the pits, Stan Hailwood hung out the sign 'Tyres OK'. When the ride was over Mike explained that he looked back because he thought he heard something flapping, but Charlie

Rous said: 'Mike eased up towards the end and we had to speed him up. He was losing the average through just getting bored. There was certainly nothing exciting about it at all. It was just high speed circulation. Once he was in top gear he just left it there. There were very few people about and it didn't look at all impressive. He was just whistling around on his own'.

Three laps from the end the MV began to misfire and on the last lap it ran out of fuel, though Hailwood was not in any fear of losing the record. Charlie Rous, who had done much to encourage Stan and Mike to go for the record and who was an expert record breaker himself, remembered the situation like this: 'The engine spluttered two or three times during the last three laps, and then on the last lap it cut dead. Mike coaxed it home and there was hardly a cupful of petrol in the tank at the end'.

It was not a triumph widely or wildly acclaimed. Bob McIntyre, who had been killed racing in 1962, was deservedly, a well-respected rider and many of his legion of fans felt that the One Hour Record, which had been an enormous feat on the Gilera three back in 1957 and on the Monza circuit, should have been left for all time as a lasting tribute to a rider of enormous talent and dedication. But Mike Hailwood, though a little embarrassed about it all and in one respect reluctant to go for the record

An 'okay' signal from father Stan Hailwood as Mike flashes to a new One Hour Record (B.R. Nicholls).

Benedicto Caldarella on the 500 cc Gilera leads Mike Hailwood on the 500 cc MV four at the United States Grand Prix at Daytona in 1964, but the Gilera later had gearbox trouble and Caldarella retired (B.R. Nicholls).

because Bob was dead and could not defend it, knew that if he did not do it, some other rider would. The other point which the critics made abundantly clear was that McIntyre had set the record at 141 mph on a 350 machine all those years ago, while Hailwood could only beat it fractionally on a 500.

Like so many of MV's triumphs over the years, the record was theirs, but they did not seem to gain a great deal of popular recognition for it. It turned out to be a day of total triumph for MV, for Hailwood went on to win the United States Grand Prix that same afternoon to make Count Agusta back in Italy a very happy man. What his reaction might have been had Mike missed the Hour Record and then failed in the US Grand Prix hardly bears thinking about. Count Agusta liked his own way, but if he was not going to have it, then the one thing that made the situation bearable was further outstanding success for MV.

Charlie Rous said there was no come back from Italy and in Domenico's peculiar way, 'he sort of congratulated us on the one hand and then said that if we had been going to do this we should have prepared a machine specially'. Really, no-one could argue with him on that.

The point to bear in mind is this: on the face of it Hailwood had an easy task. Whether he set out to demolish the record or simply exceed it, was not really considered by those who were disappointed that he did not push the record significantly higher. It is true that if MV had decided deliberately to go for the record and had prepared a machine specially for the attempt, the speed would have been much higher with, in Count Agusta's opinion, that much extra value in publicity and prestige for his factory. On the other hand, although the record books entered another success for MV, in Charlie Rous' view it was a very significant achievement which many people did not fully appreciate. He reiterated recently: 'The bike was in no way prepared for such an attempt. It really wasn't up to grand prix standards. When you consider this, it was quite an achievement really. Very much so in fact'.

The afternoon's grand prix was seen basically as an encounter between Benedicto Caldarella and Mike Hailwood riding machines from the traditional warring factories of Gilera and MV. In a way Hailwood was more equipped for the race than Caldarella. Although 125 miles round Daytona's open, banked and smooth surface could well mean a gruelling hour's ride for the less experienced

Caldarella, for Hailwood it would be probably less of a burden than a couple of laps of the TT. On the other hand, the South American would start the race completely fresh, while Hailwood might tire more easily after his morning exertions.

For something like 14 laps the Gilera and MV battled it out together, but then Hailwood moved ahead and Caldarella eventually retired when gear box trouble put the Gilera out of action. In one way it was a lucky win for MV. Almost certainly, if each rider had been on the other's bike, the decision might well have gone to Gilera, for as Charlie Rous confirmed: 'On that particular day, the Gilera was miles faster than the MV. But Hailwood outrode Caldarella with no difficulty on all but the fast, banked part of the circuit. Coming out of the twisty bit Hailwood would be right on the Gilera's tail and then as they zoomed round the banking, the Gilera would gradually pull away. The MV couldn't even stay in the Gilera's slipstream at that point, and that's a fact'.

Charlie said that Mike had commented at the time that he never dreamed that he would not be able to keep in the slipstream of another bike when he was riding an MV four, but in Rous' expert opinion, Hailwood would still have won the race, even if Caldarella had not retired. 'He would have continued to outride him anyway, though the Gilera gave Mike some concern. The banked part of the circuit was so far round that it gave the Gilera the chance to get fairly well ahead, but I think that the more Hailwood stuck his neck out, the better he did and he eventually pushed the Gilera so hard that it had to be stopped with a broken gearbox.'

Altogether it had been a good day for MV, whatever the circumstances. They went into the record books with a new One Hour Record and had moved off to a supreme start on their quest for their seventh 500 cc world title with a new race speed record for Daytona at 100.16 mph and a new record lap of 103.3 mph.

A fascinating footnote to the whole affair was pointed out by Charlie Rous. At the time of Hailwood's new record, the FIM ruling was that if a machine of lesser capacity broke a greater capacity record, then it took that record. For instance, McIntyre's One Hour Record in 1957 was on a *350 cc* Gilera, but as the speed exceeded the previous record set by Ray Amm on a *500 cc* Norton, it took the record. In 1965, however, the FIM changed the rule so that a machine could only hold a record for its own class. It could be argued that, on this basis, though the ruling came after Hailwood's new record, McIntyre's 350 cc record retains some validity.

Chapter 10

Count Domenico Agusta

It is probably true to say that even his closest associates found Count Domenico Agusta a puzzle. To those forced to make a more distant assessment, he was even more of an enigma. His passion for motor cycle racing was unquestionable. Staunchly patriotic, he made no secret of the fact that if anything gave him greater joy than seeing an MV machine win a race—and a world title—it was in seeing the honour concluded by an Italian rider.

It was his inspiration which first took MV into motor cycle production; his driving force which carried the machines he made and tuned as a hobby in a corner of his helicopter factory to the top of the world. Where other factories found the going too hard or the costs too heavy, Count Agusta's courage and obsession kept MV a racing phenomenon. As the squealing, screaming two-strokes from Japan began to envelop road racing, first in one class and then another, it was the Count's resolution which almost alone kept the full-blooded, inspiring sound of the four-stroke a feature of the grand prix circuits.

It is impossible to say how much the Count invested in racing. *Motor Cycle Weekly* editor Mick Woollett who, as sports editor of the paper, was for many years as close to racing as anyone during MV's racing heyday, once guessed it at perhaps around £2 million. It was once rumoured that the Count sold a couple of estates to keep the motor cycle side of the business going. Whatever he spent could not be justified in commercial terms, for MV's business in motor cycles was never remotely related to that kind of outlay. Yet for all his single-mindedness when it came to racing, there was something of the Jekyll and Hyde about Count Agusta. At times he would be sympathetic and understanding. At other times, stubborn and bigoted. A rider's request for what would seem to be a reasonable ride might be turned down flat without explanation. A much more difficult decision would at other times be made quickly and without fuss in the rider's favour. It was his unpredictability which confused and often enraged his riders. The Italians, not surprisingly, got along with him better than his British riders. Bill Lomas, himself a rider of strong conviction and plain words, found the relationship intolerable and quit when he could not get the Count to listen to his

demands to improve the machines. Hailwood, later, had repeated skirmishes as a result of more personal contact and found maddening the way he was often kept waiting after travelling long distances. He was once kept waiting three days for an arranged appointment and only after storming out in a rage was he called back by pursuing staff who were terrified of the consequences if Mike did not swallow his pride and return with them. On the surface he could appear bad mannered and inconsiderate, but the fact that the Count drove himself tremendously hard, day after day, chasing an impossible schedule of meetings, discussions, decisions, might have had something to do with his apparent rudeness. Another factor could have been his classic Italian aristocratic background which established and maintained a formal boss-worker relationship which by British standards was almost Victorian.

A lot has been made of Count Agusta's stubborn character and high-handed inflexibility, but it is important not to allow the picture to be tilted too far over. There was also a sympathetic and understanding side to his personality and even Hailwood,

Count Domenico Agusta in his study at Casina Costa as John Surtees signs an MV contract (Mick Woollett).

Count Agusta and the MV contingent, with three TT trophies and the Jimmy Simpson award (Mick Woollett).

at times one of his most vocal critics, admitted that he could be the most charming of men.

His unpredictability found outlet in other ways too. Although he spent a fortune sending his machines and riders to contest the grands prix in all parts of Europe and kept close tabs on race results, he seldom went to see his bikes and riders in action, except at Monza. He was a prodigious worker and virtually the whole of his life was his business. He made all the decisions and, although he spent a lot of money developing his machines and buying the best riders, he kept a tight control of the budget. His was an autocratic method of business management. He was the ultimate boss. Yet the money he pumped into racing showed that he was often ruled by his heart and not his head, so passionate was his desire to see his machines with Italian riders conquer the world.

He appeared incapable of delegation. It was quite usual for him to work well into the small hours and he would be in the office the next morning at 10.00 or 10.30. He did not seem to recognise the right of his riders to be any less dedicated. That was why they could be summoned to meet him at his office at nine or ten at night. His business was his life.

It was difficult if not impossible for any non-Italian fully to understand Count Agusta. Hailwood admitted that after four years with MV he left the factory knowing little more about the Count than when he first signed up. His attitudes and personality were too deeply rooted in the traditional Italian family background. His family were extremely wealthy landowners and much of the land surrounding the MV factory at Gallarate, including that on which Malpensa Airport stood, belonged to the Agustas. Many Italian industries were started by wealthy families and the personal rivalries which existed in the beginning were carried forward to succeeding generations. To some extent Gilera and MV were cast in this traditional Italian image, though the Gilera family were never as prosperous as the Agustas. An autocratic approach to business was often a natural feature of this heritage. Personal fortunes were used to initiate and develop businesses and for most of Count Agusta's lifetime the MV factory had no directors. It seemed natural therefore that the man who provided the cash also ran the business and made the decisions.

Physically, Count Domenico Agusta was a typical Italian, though he was born in Palermo, Sicily in 1907. Only five feet five inches tall, rugged and thick set, the pictures taken of him at Monza and at the MV factory during the 1960s often showed him in a long coat and wide brimmed hat. 'Straight from the Mafia', someone joked at the time: but of course, *most* Italians looked that way in those days. He spoke rapidly in disjointed phrases and although he was said to speak no English, some of his closer associates reckoned he understood English reasonably well and could even speak it tolerably.

There is no doubt that he was tough and unyielding. He ruled MV from a position of strength. When things went wrong or jobs were not completed in time he would get very angry. His employees feared being called into his office for they knew that in most cases such an order was the prelude to an angry scene. His decision was final. His desk was built up on a platform so that once seated in his swivel chair he could look down on visitors and maintain a psychological advantage. His office was by no means plush. His machines raced all over Europe, in Britain and America, but the Count hardly moved out of Gallarate. He kept in touch by closely scrutinising the race results and reports and through the battery of telephones near to his desk. He used a radio-telephone for up-to-date reports on the helicopter business.

Count Agusta's private villa was set in the grounds of the factory complex which, in the peak days of MV racing, was a sprawl of buildings well guarded by patrols. When his machines won races he would be quiet and content. A defeat or a breakdown inevitably prompted a major inquiry with the Count personally driving his staff into action. One of the tales told by Hailwood concerns the MV's ignominious defeat at the hands of Gilera at Imola in 1963. It was difficult for Count Agusta to accept defeat anywhere, but at Monza or Imola before an Italian crowd he accepted anything short of total triumph as absolute disaster. Geoff Duke's plan had brought the 1957 Gileras once more to the track and Derek Minter and John Hartle on the Gileras faced Mike Hailwood on the MV on what was looked upon as a trial of strength and a definite pointer to the grand prix season to come. Mike had crashed at Brands Hatch before the Italian race and was still being troubled by a damaged wrist. After two laps he was in considerable pain and although he continued for eight more laps, during which time he kept ahead of the Gileras, the wrist finally gave out and he could do little as Minter and Hartle raced ahead to take first and second place.

According to Hailwood, the Count saw the race on television at his villa and was furious at the defeat by, of all factories, the arch rival Gilera. He had Hailwood in the office next morning and gave Mike no chance to explain. He stormed at Hailwood, saying he should have retired from the race rather than allow the Gileras to beat him. The outburst was so venomous that Mike lost his temper and, as he explained later, 'I yelled back at him and said that if he thought he could do any better he should ride the bloody thing himself, and strode out'.

After an hour Count Agusta telephoned Hailwood's hotel and invited him back for a chat. Said Mike: 'He was full of charm and apologies'. This was indeed a respectful gesture from Domenico who, other associates have agreed, found it difficult to apologise whatever the circumstances.

Though he kept a personal control on the money being spent, this is not to say that he was ungenerous. He did not waste money knowingly but, when the occasion demanded it, would agree to considerable expenditure. If he personally wanted something to happen then he would pay almost anything. Indeed, some riders criticised him for buying off the opposition—quoting Les Graham, Provini, Ray Amm and Gary Hocking, as riders having been lured to MV by profitable contracts. Certainly, in those days of the middle and late 1950s riders were expected to race for British factories more for the honour than the money. By that comparison Count Agusta 'bought' success but, in the light of what happened in the 1960s and '70s, you could say he was an entrepreneur in this field—the first of the big spenders.

Count Agusta was a remote, mysterious figure and his relationships with riders were generally formal. Curiously, it was with his first British rider, Les Graham, that he was on the most informal terms. Les used to chat away in pigeon Italian and the Count would listen and be prepared to accept advice about machine modifications and other aspects of racing. No other rider ever got quite as close to the Count. Les's son Stuart feels that at the time the Count was in need of Graham's advice and experience as much as Les needed the works contract which was on offer from MV; it was this mutual need which at first brought them close together. Later the Count was able to be more independent and could dictate the way things should go.

In some respects, though it is a personal view, history has not been too kind or over-just to Count Domenico Agusta. The MV machines which he created set an incomparable record in World Championship racing, the grand prix of the sport, yet his critics prefer to concentrate on the fact that

Domenico Agusta studies his latest six-cylinder MV (Mick Woollett).

many of his victories were cheaply won against little opposition. It was almost as if he had been responsible himself for the retirement from racing of other factories who could have given the MVs a much tougher ride. The alternative would have been to pull out himself—in which case international racing would have surely been much worse off and might even have collapsed altogether, temporarily. Some felt it was wrong that he should 'buy' success by signing on the best riders. But is that not what racing is all about—the best machines and the best riders?

He was criticised for not getting out and about to the race circuit more, where people could see and identify him. The difficult side of his personality was what tended to receive the publicity.

However, racing in the 1960s would have been dismal indeed in the 500 cc class without Count Agusta and his beautiful, powerful, red-tanked MV machines. They may not have been the fastest bikes ever, but they were among the most reliable over a very long time.

In 1971, within days of his 64th birthday, Count Domenico Agusta suffered a heart attack and died in Milan. With him died the greatest deeds of MV, for without his drive, passionate interest in motor cycle racing and abounding energy which he gave selflessly to the cause, MV's days as a bike racing factory were numbered. Some would claim they probably were anyway. The difference was that the Count's death removed all doubt.

As an epitaph, let us remember the kinder side of Count Domenico Agusta, recalled in the words of Mike Hailwood in the book he wrote with Ted Macauley and called, simply, *Hailwood*. Wrote Mike: 'When he's in an expansive and kindly mood he can be the epitome of charm. I remember, for instance, an occasion in 1965 when I was flying off to the Argentine Grand Prix and had to break my journey in Italy. I landed at Linate and had to get to Malpensa, about 40 miles away, for the connection. It meant a long journey by coach or taxi and a four-hour wait for the flight.

'When I flew into Linate there was a chauffeur-driven car supplied by the Count waiting for me at the airport. It whisked Stan and me off to the MV factory, where the Count had laid on a champagne snack; it was ten o'clock at night but he was still working. He had a contract ready that he wanted me to sign for the following season. He dictated the terms, which were extremely generous, and added that he was insuring me for £10,000. An hour and a half later he had put us back in the car and we were off, business finished, to the airport. It was there, I suppose, that I finally made up my mind not to switch over completely to cars.

'Somehow the Count had found out that I was on that particular aircraft and was making sure he got hold of me to sign the contract. It was a pleasant surprise to me. I had grown used to his off-hand attitude and now I was seeing the other side of him.'

Chapter 11

The Honda-Hailwood challenge

Count Domenico Augsta was an instinctive patriot and an intensely proud man. His deep, enduring satisfaction in seeing an Italian motor cycle win the most prestigious 500 cc world title an incredible nine years out of ten, was only second in importance to the fact that his own MV machinery had done the great deed. That added a kind of divine dimension to the achievement.

However, what the Count wanted most of all was to see an *Italian* ride the MV to the premier championship. That came in 1966. By then the engagingly handsome Giacomo Agostini was proving his early promise so that when Mike Hailwood 'defected' to Honda, the Count was ready to pin all his hopes on Agostini.

On paper Hailwood's switch was a disaster for MV. He had won them the title for the past four years and was the undisputed giant among riders. However, the Japanese factories were then at their peak, backing their racing effort with huge sums of money. They monopolised the grands prix and in 1965, except in the 500 cc class, captured all solo World Championships.

When the mighty Honda declared their intention of going for the 500 title and signed Hailwood to a fat and exclusive contract, the combination looked

Before Hailwood 'defected' to Honda and the 'master' shows 'pupil' Agostini the way round Sachsenring in the East German Grand Prix of 1965 (Mick Woollett).

invincible. The future bristled with adventure and excitement as Agostini was upgraded to MV's number one rider and the Count decided to stand firm and fight Honda for the title.

At the time much was made of Hailwood's move; more precisely, whether he would go to Honda or stay with MV. But anyone with even a sniff of what was going on behind the scenes might have forecast the outcome accurately. For a start Hailwood had ridden MV to success for four years, often against rather tame opposition. So on that basis alone he was perhaps overdue for the stimulus of a move. Nor did he keep his feelings secret among those close to him about the way Count Agusta was grooming Agostini for stardom. He recognised the signs as he was asked to let Agostini win a couple of races so that he could take the Italian championship. Mike was also downright angry at a similar suggestion before a race at San Remo. Hailwood's defiance counted for nothing in the end, because the MV finally let him down mechanically.

Another point in favour of a move was that Honda could offer him more rides, since they would be contesting the 250, 350 and 500 cc classes, while MV were interested only in 350 and 500 cc races.

Mike Hailwood with MV mechanic Carruana (B.R. Nicholls).

All it needed was for Honda to offer a good contract. They did and the switch was made. It was the prelude to a couple of seasons of really classic

An early MV ride for Mike Hailwood at Brands Hatch, Easter 1958 (B.R. Nicholls).

500 cc racing as MV battled to keep the title. The keen rivalry brought the championship to life with some incredible duels, but MV managed to retain the title in 1966 partly thanks to a new three-cylinder machine developed from the factory's 350 cc model; but also to politics inside the Honda camp which deprived Hailwood of a ride in the opening round in Germany and saddled him with a bike which developed gearbox trouble in the second grand prix in Holland. There was a grandstand finish to the season, the championship being decided at Monza in the last round.

The season started on a high note for Honda. Redman took the race at Hockenheim without trouble, but in the Dutch TT in July, Agostini, riding for the first time the enlarged three-cylinder MV with a capacity of about 420 cc, shocked the Honda camp. Redman admitted after the race that Honda's superiority in the previous round was so convincing that he thought the Japanese factory would have the fastest 500 for at least the next five years. 'But MV have shot that idea down in only six weeks,' he declared. At the start the Honda captain raced into the lead, but Agostini blasted the MV in pursuit and moved to the front on the second lap.

Hailwood, who did not even race the 500 in the West German opening round at Hockenheim because there was only one machine available and Redman took it, started badly when the Honda refused to fire immediately, but he closed fast on the leaders and smashed his own MV lap record by over four seconds at 92.31 mph. Meanwhile, Agostini was pulling steadily away from Redman and looked set for a surprise win until the determined Redman, who had been chipping the odd seconds off the Italian's lead, finally overtook him on lap 17. Still Agostini almost lifted the race for MV, overtaking Redman. It took a new record race speed for the Rhodesian to finish first, overtaking the MV once again with just two laps to go.

Although Hailwood had gone to Honda specifically to win them the 500 cc title, he found himself at first playing second fiddle to his team mate and friend Jim Redman. Redman, approaching the end of his racing days, was intent on adding the 500 cc crown to the four 350 cc and two 250 cc titles he had already secured for Honda in a distinguished racing career and, as team captain, he established the tactics accordingly.

The fact that Redman had elected to make himself the number one rider in the 500 cc class was against Honda's original plan, but they felt disinclined to argue the point too forcefully once

The fabulous MV four which dominated the 500 cc class for so many years (Mick Woollett).

Redman had beaten Agostini in Germany and Holland and looked well on the way to the title. The championship was their objective and whether Hailwood or Redman brought it to them was unimportant.

On the eve of the third round in Belgium, MV were struggling, but it was on the ultra-fast Francorchamps circuit that fortune turned towards the Italians. As Redman crashed heavily on a rain-soaked circuit, Agostini raced on to MV's first classic win of the season. Redman's injury put him out of effective action for the remainder of the season and he was, that very season, to retire. Hailwood, already heavily committed as the spearhead of Honda's assault on the 250 and 350 cc championships, was now forced to take up the running in the 500 cc class.

It was a monumental task, even for Hailwood. Against the old MV there is hardly a doubt that Honda would have taken the title, even after Redman's unfortunate crash, but Honda, curiously for the normally secretive Japanese, had done their cause little good by letting it be known before the season opened that they would have a 100 hp 500 ready to spearhead their challenge. Count Agusta was alerted to the threat and Mike Hailwood's signing for Honda was all that was needed to convince him that something special was required if MV had to be in with a chance of retaining the championship.

He responded by introducing a completely new three-cylinder MV. The machine had been on the

At the TTs of 1967—the three-cylinder MV. Agostini's 500 cc four reserve bike is seen at the back (Mick Woollett).

stocks for some time but, because there had been little opposition until now, the factory had not completed its development. It was an impressive machine, and, once race-prepared, only about a couple of mph slower than the Honda with much superior handling. The machine was to prove so reliable that out of the nine championship races in which it was entered, only once was Agostini forced to retire, when he crashed while leading the East German Grand Prix.

So the battle was resumed at Sachsenring. Agostini won the 350 cc race after duelling with Hailwood for more than half of the 18 laps and set a new lap record for the circuit of 107.29 mph. He seemed set to make it an impressive double by winning the 500 cc event. Hailwood had shown his determination in practice by breaking the three-minute barrier for the circuit at 2 mins 58.5 secs and

beating his old MV lap best by 8 secs. Agostini's best was 3 mins 3.4 secs, but as he had shown before, Agostini could get the MV moving quickly under the stimulus and demands of the race itself. He gained 20 yards on Hailwood's Honda in the dash to the first bend and seemed assured of victory as the Honda broke down after only five laps, trying to stay with the flashing MV. But after increasing the lap record for the 5.43 mile circuit to 107.77 mph, oil on the rear tyre of the MV brought disaster on the 120 mph downhill curve of the East German circuit. The crash wrecked the bike and the race had an unexpected winner in Frantisek Stastny on a 440 cc Jawa. Agostini, miraculously, escaped serious injury. So fast was his MV that he had lapped all the remaining riders by the time he crashed.

The rest of the season was an intensely close-fought battle. Hailwood won, with Agostini second, in Czechoslovakia. In Finland the positions were reversed. Hailwood won again in Northern Ireland, with Agostini second: and yet again in the Isle of Man TT, delayed until September in 1966 because of a seamen's strike. Here Agostini had the consolation of becoming the first continental rider ever to win the Junior TT. With the three-cylinder MV he shattered Hailwood's lap record at 103.09 mph and averaged 100.87 mph to beat Redman's race record. In the Senior event the 420 cc unit used in the MV until then was replaced by a full 500 cc engine and for three laps the MV made the Honda machine fight hard, but eventually finished second. Although it failed to bring MV victory, it was kept for the Italian Grand Prix at Monza. The final round was the decider and in front of an ecstatic home crowd Agostini took the MV to the all-important win, while buckled valves on the big Honda caused Hailwood to retire.

It had been a brilliant season for MV and the handsome young Italian's meteoric rise to fame made him perhaps the biggest name in racing in 1966. Among a collection of non-championship races in Italy and Britain during the year he rode the latest three-cylinder 350 at Modena in March to thrash conclusively a powerful challenge from Remo Venturi on a 500 cc Gilera making its first appearance since 1964. The MV led from beginning to end in this first race of the Italian championships and smashed both race and lap records.

A month later the overbored 350 MV cracked Mike Hailwood's lap record at Rimini, but then 'blew up', when leading the 500 cc race.

Agostini's 1966 world title was the beginning of a brilliant career in which he was to amass more World Championships than any other rider—all except one on MV machinery.

He had started racing in 1963 and after a series of hill-climbs and national road race successes on his own 175 cc Morini, the young grand prix challenger only rode his first major race that same year, when he was forced to retire his works Morini in the Italian Grand Prix after taking the lead on the first lap. Replacing Tarquinio Provini as Morini's number one rider in 1964, Agostini's success in winning the 250 cc Italian championship brought him to the attention of Count Agusta, who signed him as support rider to Mike Hailwood in the MV Agusta team for 1965. Despite his lack of experience, his success in the World Championship series was immediate. Though he had never before ridden anything bigger than a 250, he finished runner-up to Hailwood in the 500 cc class and was denied the 350 cc world title when a contact-breaker spring broke while he was leading the Japanese

Grand Prix. At the end of the season he was only six points short of World Champion Jim Redman's total.

The Count's faith in his young prodigy had been fully justified and the Italian race baron—over-joyed at MV's first 500 cc World Championship won by an Italian—now gave his consent for Agostini to appear in major end-of-season races in England. Making his short circuit debut at Britain's celebrated Mallory Park, Agostini had a field day, thrilling 50,000 spectators and taking MV to victory in all the five races contested, including what was then the richest race in Britain, the £1,050 first prize 'Race of the Year'. In the big-money race, however, luck was on the Italian's side. Hailwood, after making a brilliant start on the 250 cc six-cylinder Honda, was leading by ten seconds with just seven laps to go, when his rear tyre was punctured. On the celebrated three-cylinder MV, Agostini had been boxed in at the start and had to fight his way through the field for 12 laps. He equalled Hailwood's old MV lap record at 91.69 mph and reduced Mike's lead from 14 to ten seconds, but it is fair to say that his task was hopeless until the Honda's puncture which left the MV a clear field.

Such was Agostini's box office appeal that he was reported to have received, for his visit to Mallory, the highest start money ever paid to a rider competing in a British motor cycle meeting.

An MV warning signal to Hailwood (now Honda-mounted) during the Senior TT of 1967 (Mick Woollett).

At the end of 1966 there were strong rumours that Count Agusta had decided to expand his racing effort for 1967 and that he was almost certain to sign on a second string to give Agostini support in the World Championships. Renzo Pasolini was reckoned to be first choice, but the contract did not materialise.

When the World Championship trail was resumed in 1967, it was no surprise to find Agostini back in the MV saddle. There were also rumours about a possible return to MV by Hailwood, and unconfirmed reports that Count Agusta had made an indirect approach. Hailwood's contract with Honda had been for just the one year and it was plain that he was disappointed with certain aspects of Honda's strategy and had often been angry with the big Honda's poor handling. With Hailwood and Agostini riding MVs, Count Agusta would almost certainly have been assured of both the 350 and 500 cc world titles, but in the end Hailwood continued to ride the Honda in the 500 cc class, a

decision influenced perhaps by the opportunity to ride Honda machines in the 250 and 350 cc classes.

By now MV had won the 500 cc World Championship nine years in succession and Count Agusta was determined to fight any threatened move which might deny him the title for a tenth time. His crystal-clear objective, which also included Agostini contesting the 350 cc class, was in sharp contrast to Honda's widespread commitment, which until 1967, had found them battling in all solo classes. They were worried that their prodigious investment in developing four-, five- and six-cylinder racers had failed to discourage the insistent two-stroke challenge from Yahama and Suzuki in the lower capacity classes. At the same time, European racing was beginning to make less sense commercially as the vast potential of the United States opened up with the surging interest there in motor cycles.

So for 1967 Honda took the hard decision, cut back their racing effort, pulled out of 50 cc and 125

Agostini on the MV leads Hailwood on the Honda during the 500 cc race at the Dutch TT of 1967, but Hailwood beat Agostini to the finishing line (Mick Woollett).

Agostini races the MV to victory in the 500 cc Belgian Grand Prix of 1967 (Mick Woollett).

cc racing completely, but agreed to support Mike Hailwood and Ralph Bryans with existing machines in the three bigger classes.

It had been around April 1966 that the first rumours of Agostini's completely new 500 MV for 1967 began to circulate. According to one report MV had started work on the machine some time before but had not considered its development as a matter of urgency because of the lack of opposition to Hailwood. Now, with Hailwood riding for Honda, work on the machine had been accelerated.

As the new racing season opened there was a psychological boost for MV as Agostini, saving the new three-cylinder 500 for the more important West German Grand Prix to come, shattered the absolute lap record in the 500 cc race of the Austrian Grand Prix at Salzburg, a non-championship event, *on the old machine.*

On the new machine, which was a three-cylinder model with twin overhead cam and improved frame, MV hopes soared even more as Agostini won the opening round at Hockenheim but Honda countered with wins by Hailwood on the Isle of Man and in Holland. On the Isle of Man the MV was one of only three machines to hurtle through the speed trap at more than 150 mph during practice, Agostini being the fastest at 155.2 mph. The Senior TT was an exciting battle as both the MV and Honda lapped at more than 108 mph, the lap record being smashed repeatedly. With over two laps to go, Agostini was two seconds ahead of Hailwood and looked certain to win. Then the rear chain jumped the sprockets, broke and Hailwood raced the Honda to victory. Agostini beat Hailwood in Belgium and at Sachsenring in East Germany. Hailwood won in Czechoslovakia but it was clear during the season that he had generally been unhappy with the poor handling of the Honda. He even got brake expert Colin Lyster to build him a new frame in which he planned to put the 500 cc

73

engine but the company in Japan vetoed the idea, insisting that the grand prix machine should be a Honda thoroughbred. Agostini won in Finland, Hailwood once more in Northern Ireland and so, with two rounds left, the battling giants travelled to Monza for what was once again to turn out to be the season's deciding race. Hailwood should have won, which would have taken the world title from MV, but with a lead of half a lap over Agostini and just two laps from the finish, the Honda's gearbox refused to function and Agostini was able to take the MV into the lead to win.

Hailwood beat Agostini in the final round in Canada but the result made no difference to the outcome of the championship. The competition had been closer than ever, the rivalry more intense and, in a nerve-tingling, cliff-hanging climax the 500 cc World Championship went once again to MV and Agostini. Both riders had 46 points, but Agostini took the title because of his three second-place positions against Hailwood's two.

It was MV's 25th world title in just 15 years of competition, during which time they had also won a total of 160 World Championship races. Of these 70 had been in the premier 500 cc class.

Then without warning came Honda's shock decision. Hailwood was summoned to Japan in February 1968 thinking it was to test machines for the new season. Instead he was told that Honda had decided to quit motor cycle racing to concentrate on the development of their Formula 1 car and that he was out of a job. MV had denied Honda their one remaining ambition in grand prix racing—the 500 cc World Championship—and the Italian factory was left virtually without opposition to make the 500 cc world title their own in the longest run of success ever achieved by any factory.

Those highly competitive two seasons were golden days for 500 cc racing and were perhaps MV's most glorious years, for they became the only factory which Honda just could not beat, even with superstar Hailwood riding.

Chapter 12

Agostini—a new king at MV

After 1967 there was hardly any opposition to MV in the heavier classes for six years. Hailwood had the use of the '67 Honda during 1968, but was paid a handsome sum not to ride in the classic events. Honda had their pride. They were not prepared to give an all-out assault on the 500 cc title the investment it required to face MV competitively again. Technically Hailwood was given a choice, but the contract offered to him not to compete in championship races was so much better than the alternative, which would have allowed him to contest the championship again, that he made the obvious decision and rode the Honda in international and other important non-title events only. He was not all that bothered anyway, since his ambitions had already shifted to car racing and he was to retire from motor cycle sport at the end of the year.

A lot of the interest in grand prix racing switched to the 125 and 250 cc classes, with the sensational scrap between Phil Read and Bill Ivy riding Yamahas grabbing the headlines. It began as friendly rivalry, developed into a bitter struggle and ended in the sensational and now well-documented feud. To ride the unchanged racers Agostini was MV's natural choice. With only privately entered Matchless machines ridden by Jack Findlay and Switzerland's Marsovszky providing any kind of challenge in the 500 cc class, and Renzo Pasolini and Kel Carruthers (Aermacchi) struggling hopelessly in the 350 cc class, it came as no surprise when MV collected both world titles by a wide margin of points. The MVs were so far ahead of the opposition that Agostini was able to win all seven 350 and all ten 500 cc championship rounds. It was a record never before achieved in the history of the World Championships. It is easy to remember that MV gained this distinction against little opposition, but the MV's reliability and Agostini's remarkable consistency should not be forgotten.

Like so much else in motor cycle racing, it remains an interesting speculation whether MV would have taken the world titles again had Honda decided to give the championship one more try. The protagonists came together at Rimini in the important pre-championship races and Hailwood had the better of both the 350 and 500 cc encounters. Honda's interest in motor cycle racing

had flagged, so Hailwood was allowed to go ahead and work on the frame problems which had made the Honda so difficult to handle in previous years. Ken Sprayson of Reynolds Tubes designed and built a brand new, three-down tube frame, completing the work only a week before the Rimini races. Mike used it for the first time in the 500 event and although he completed only a few practice laps, he was able to lead Agostini on the MV commandingly for the first ten laps of the 28-lap race. The new frame gave the Honda greater stability and he looked set to win. Then Hailwood tweaked the twist grip too heavily on a slippery corner and came off, the mistake setting him back a full half minute. He remounted and, in spite of a broken windscreen, pushed the lap record for the tricky two-mile circuit to 83.79 mph. He finished second to Agostini in spite of a mishap, while Agostini gave his fans heart failure as he unaccountably shot up a slip road, which almost cost him the

Giacomo Agostini who, after Hailwood's departure to Honda, became MV's top rider during their most successful years (B.R. Nicholls).

Agostini (8) pushes off the MV alongside Derek Minter with the Norton at the start of the Senior race on his first visit to the Isle of Man, in 1965. He retired (B.R. Nicholls).

race. The reason was a new front brake on the MV which had been successfully tested at Monza and Modena, but which did not stand up quite as well to the notorious demands on brakes made by the tight Rimini circuit. It was a discouraging day for Agostini and the MV camp, for the Honda six made the smaller MV look slow in the 350 cc race, with Hailwood winning easily before 30,000 of Agostini's Italian compatriots.

The Rimini results caused concern at Gallarate. The danger was that Honda, sniffing the possibility that they might still be able to take the championship away from the Italian factory without having to develop their machines further, might make an 11th hour switch of tactics and decide to contest the championships after all. Nor was there much consolation for MV after the rivals clashed again in the second Italian non-championship meeting at Cesenatico. In a remarkable tearaway 350 cc event, Hailwood crashed the 297 cc Honda six, but Agostini could not keep the MV going at the same pace as a rocketing Benelli ridden by Pasolini and, while the results showed that the MV won the 500 cc race, a downpour took the competitive edge off the event so that Agostini came home first mainly because of the MV's more reliable handling in poor conditions.

Rumours were now rife. It seemed for a while that Honda might respond and put Hailwood back into the championship fight. Meanwhile, MV, alert to the danger, were advancing their programme of development on new 350 and 500 cc racers for Agostini, with the greatest urgency being given to the 350 cc project. Agostini had already admitted publicly that it was impossible for him to beat the Honda in this class with the present three-cylinder MV. After Pasolini's impressive outing at Cesenatico, MV looked like having a tough ride against the Benelli works machines which were going for the 350 title. They were certainly faster than the MV 350 presently bring ridden by Agostini and would probably have the edge on a new 350 which was already completed back at the factory. MV team manager Arturo Magni confirmed that work was going on to provide Agostini with new racers but, as time drew near for the opening round of the 1968 championships at Nürburgring, Hailwood said he had still heard nothing from Japan and Benelli emerged as MV's major threat in classic racing.

Permission from Honda was never received and the rivalry with MV continued only in non-championship races. In April Honda had the better of things at Imola with Hailwood sweeping to victory in the 500 cc event on his special-framed Honda, crossing the line almost 20 seconds ahead of Agostini.

As hopes faded of a Honda return, MV saw the challenge of Benelli, with works racers, as their major threat. Their chance in the 350 cc race at the Nürburgring in the West German Grand Prix, the season's curtain raiser, was taken seriously because the Benelli was recognised even in the MV camp as being faster than Agostini's machine. Pasolini was a flyer, though Agostini held some advantage in having raced at the notorious Nürburgring before, where in 1965 he had won his first classic race for MV on the then new three-cylinder machine.

Although MV sources insisted that the factory was working hard on a completely new machine for the 350 cc class, nothing appeared for the opening round and it was left to the MV tuners to squeeze a fraction more power out of the existing 350 three by improving carburation. This was sufficient for Agostini to beat off the Benelli challenge in the 350 cc race. In the 500 cc event Dan Shorey on a Norton led a pack of privately-entered machines home to finish second to the MV, which was really in a class of its own.

Agostini won the second 500 cc round in Spain and then prepared for the Isle of Man. Count Agusta saw the TT races as vital to the taking of the world titles and recognised the need to provide Agostini with some back up. The TT course is demanding in a different way from any other grand prix circuit and it only needed Agostini to retire with mechanical trouble or to make an error of judgement and MV's chances of adding valuable championship points at a psychologically important stage in the series would be gone.

Machine competition to MV may not have been all that strong but the Count was certainly keeping the championships alive as he offered bikes to a number of riders. Former World Champion Jim Redman, who had retired to South Africa after his bad crash at the Belgian Grand Prix in 1966, had been itching to race again and wrote to MV to see if they could supply a machine for the Italian Grand Prix later in the season. Instead they offered him a works bike for the TT and Redman had his bags packed and was set to fly to England when he received a telegram saying he would not be able to get an entry.

Stuart Graham, racing son of former MV star Les Graham, was also offered a three-cylinder 350 for the TT but entries had closed by the time the offer arrived. Stuart commented recently: 'I got on to the A-CU right away, but it was no good. They turned me down because the entry was late'. Stuart said he would have loved to have ridden an MV, particularly in view of his father's earlier connection with the factory. MV also said they would provide a machine for Mike Hailwood, whose contract with Honda prevented him for riding the Japanese machines in the TT championship races, but eventually the support they got for Agostini was in the form of talented racer John Hartle. Hartle's successful partnering of John Surtees in the MV-dominated days of 1958 and '59 was remembered by MV again now. As reported earlier, fearsome crashes had punctuated Hartle's career but had not dented his courage. He relished the opportunity of riding something quick again, since he had only ridden single-cylinder machines since racing the Gilera fours under the Geoff Duke banner in 1963. He quickly answered Count Agusta's telegram which invited him to state his terms and conditions. Following his come-back to racing the previous year, Hartle knew this to be his big chance and he was eager to take it.

He was expected to have a three-cylinder machine for the Junior event and one of the older, slower fours for the Senior. Hartle was not daunted by the possibility of being hired to ride second to the Count's number one rider, Agostini. He had taken over the 'bridesmaid' role in 1958 and '59 when he had been engaged as support rider to John Surtees, whose outstanding form and strong championship challenge made him the more important MV property. Hartle might well have felt that the position now was similar, but with Agostini occupying the 'superstar' billing. But although Count Agusta said nothing, Agostini insisted that Hartle be given his head. 'So much can happen in the TT and it is important only that MV should win, especially in the 350 cc race where we must beat Renzo Pasolini and the Benelli', he said; though it was clear that Agostini would ride the faster machine. The tactics in the more

Agostini in command of the 350 cc MV at Rimini in March 1968 (Mick Woollett).

At the Nürburgring, Agostini leads Pasolini on the Benelli at the West German Grand Prix of 1968 (Mick Woollett).

threatening Junior race would be for Hartle to try to hang on to Agostini and thereby make things difficult for Pasolini on the Benelli. Riding the MV again, Hartle described his feelings as a mixture of trepidation and exhilaration. 'But it is great to be on something with urge, real urge I mean', he said. Sadly, his first outing on the 500 MV in practice on the Saturday morning ended prematurely with John pushing in after three laps, the chain coming off at Signpost Corner. Even so, his enthusiasm was obvious and his views were by no means unique among MV-experienced racers when he commented before the race: 'The MV is such a good bike that it is difficult to compare anything with it. It is so comfortable, handles so well, and is so easy to ride that you cannot help feeling instantly at home on it'.

MV had seven machines on the island—two three-cylinder 500s, three 350s and two four-cylinder 500s. Agostini's 350 machine was new with a disc brake at the front but, as Agostini lacked experience of hydraulic disc brakes, he was expected to revert to normal brakes for the race.

Agostini was certainly at home on the MV. He set the pace in early training sessions, tearing round the Mountain Course at 103.84 mph. Pasolini was only

a few seconds slower at 102.31 mph and Hartle, quickly settling down on the powerful works machine, was moving near to the 100 mph mark when flies on the windscreen forced him to slow down. Everything pointed to a thrilling and closely contested Junior TT as Agostini and Hartle later took the MVs round the course faster than ever before and Hartle's performance was all the more creditable since his machine was considerably over-geared.

However Hartle's 'dream' return to MV turned into a nightmare. He managed only one lap in the Senior race before crashing, and a spill in the relatively unimportant production event on a British machine put him out of the Junior TT altogether. Agostini was the hero. During the Senior TT he took the MV through the Highlander speed trap at 157.9 mph, the highest speed ever recorded there and 3.4 mph faster than the previous best set by Mike Hailwood on the 500 cc four-cylinder Honda. He won both the Senior and Junior TTs to score an amazing double, at the same time setting the fastest laps in both races. In the Junior event he led all the way and with Hartle out of the race and the expected challenge from the Benelli of Pasolini never really developing, he had little to worry about. He was an incredible 36 seconds ahead at the end of the first lap and on all six laps he rushed the impressive MV three through the *Motor Cycle News* speed trap on the stretch between Greg ny Baa and Brandish Corner at more than 140 mph—146.3, 145.2, 141.7, 142.5, 144.0 and 140.6 mph. And he smashed Mike Hailwood's Junior race record at a speed of 104.78 mph.

On a personal note it was some consolation for the crushing disappointment he had felt on his Isle of Man debut the previous year when he lost to Hailwood when he might so easily have won. It was Agostini's first Senior TT victory and his first Isle of Man double. It was also the first time an Italian had won the Senior TT. These victories put MV in a good position in the World Championship with maximum points in both classes.

In Holland the MVs were once more invincible though in the 350 cc race Agostini fought off a challenge from Bultaco rider Ginger Molloy. In retrospect this was an interesting clash because it was to be the New Zealand rider who provided a challenge to Agostini in the 500 cc class two years later when MV were even more solidly entrenched as the world leaders in big bike racing. Then the Japanese were challenging through the new Kawasaki factory. Had they given more support to either Ginger Molloy, or Dave Simmons, who brought them a World Championship in the 125 cc

Above *John Hartle astride the works three-cylinder MV during TT practice in 1968. A crash in the production event prevented him from riding the MV in the race (Mick Woollett).* **Below** *In 1968 Agostini and MV won every 350 and 500 cc grand prix—17 races in all. They are seen leading Pagani, Carruthers and Milani in the 350 cc race of the Czechoslovakian round (Mick Woollett).*

Time for a chat. Agostini (3) on the MV and Hailwood on the Honda at Mallory Park (Mick Woollett).

class in 1969, MV's passage to yet another title in the 500 cc class would have been much harder, for the 500 cc Kawasaki could really travel fast.

As the riders made their way to Assen the 350 cc championship battle was very much alive, only four points separating Agostini on the MV and Pasolini on the Benelli. But Pasolini's crash on the third lap in Holland badly damaged the Benelli and although he re-mounted and got back in the race without losing his place, he crashed again on the next lap and retired, allowing the MV to move 12 clear points ahead.

With three straight wins in the first three rounds. Agostini only had to win in the fourth round in East Germany to make the 500 cc World Championship his for the third time in succession and to give MV the title for an impressive 12 times. He did it in the most powerful way with a new absolute lap record of 109.79 mph. The MV's disc brakes which had been tried in practice were discarded for the race and the MV three ran faultlessly, a fine tribute to

the watching mechanics. Agostini's cornering in brilliant weather before 200,000 spectators at the exciting Sachsenring circuit was a joy to watch. He seemed totally in tune with the machine and by also winning the 350 cc event, in which he looked set to smash the class lap record until a patch of oil on a corner slowed him down, he seemed well on the way to becoming the first Italian to take the double 350 and 500 cc World Championships.

The combination of MV and Agostini stormed on relentlessly—Czechoslovakia, Finland, Ulster: but the predictable nature of 500 cc results was jolted out of its blandness when Count Agusta woke everyone up for the final grand prix of the year at Monza. By now the championships were his, so the outcome of the Italian Grand Prix was purely academic. Speculation and excitement rose when MV race manager Arturo Magni telephoned Mike Hailwood and offered him an MV for Monza. The surprise move followed Hailwood's outstanding performances in the Hutchinson 100 at Brands

Hatch the previous day when he shattered top class opposition in the form of Renzo Pasolini, Bill Ivy and Phil Read. Mike, still the reigning 250 and 350 cc World Champion, continued to command huge respect as a rider although not competing in the classic rounds on the Honda, and the MV offer almost coincided with a similar approach from Benelli.

The reason for MV's approach was that the long-awaited 350, now being rumoured as a six-cylinder machine, would be wheeled out for the home crowd's benefit at Monza and Count Agusta wanted two riders in the class, one to ride the new machine and the other the current three-cylinder world beater. Redman was also keen to ride MV at Monza and waiting on the sidelines, should Hailwood decline, was the Australian Jack Findlay, who had caught MV's eye with a brilliant season and was at that time lying second in the 500 cc World Championship.

Hailwood desperately wanted to ride—and win—at Monza for he had old scores to settle with Agostini who, remember, had won the battle to retain the championship over Hailwood's Honda challenge in both 1966 and '67 at the famous Italian circuit. As in previous years Monza was the scene of unexpected drama and sensation. Hailwood agreed to ride for MV and after he had shown the quality of his challenge in practice by knocking six tenths of a second off Ralph Bryans 1967 Monza record of 121.61 mph, the dramas began. Count Agusta instructed Hailwood to let Agostini win in both races if it became a choice between the two riders. Hailwood flatly refused. On the day before Sunday's race, Mike stood firm. The Count partially conceded and said he would permit Hailwood to win the 350 race. Hailwood was adamant. He was intent on overcoming his Monza bogey and proving himself a better rider than Agostini. He told the MV boss that the chance of winning just one race was not enough. He had to be in with an equal chance against Agostini in both races or he would not race at all. The Count might have thought he was bluffing but Mike showed he was not by packing his belongings ready for a return to England. Then, seeing an opportunity, Benelli stepped in and offered Mike their new four-cylinder 500. Hailwood accepted and excitement mounted as he equalled the 500 lap record on the new Benelli during the three-lap practice session.

The race started and the two giants of motor cycle racing were once more locked in battle. The tension was intense as Hailwood and Agostini raced together round the famous circuit, the excitable Italians shouting for their national hero. Then, on a rain soaked circuit, Hailwood's Monza jinx struck again. Dicing with Agostini on the South Curve on the third lap, he overdid things and parted company from the Benelli. Agostini stormed ahead to take the race and complete a fine double victory for MV after also winning the 350 cc event.

An interesting sideline to the Hailwood offer from MV almost gave Australian Kel Carruthers a chance to ride for the famous factory. When Mike sent a telegram saying he would he happy to accept their offer, the MV factory at first misunderstood the wording and began looking around for another rider and approached Kel Carruthers. Not until Mike arrived in Italy did MV learn that he intended riding for them and a disappointed Carruthers had to be content with a works Aermacchi in the 350 cc race.

The formidable combination of MV and Agostini capped a sensational season of racing by smashing Remo Venturi's old MV Privat record at the San Remo circuit in October. The new record lap at 62.9 mph helped Agostini to a 20 second win in the combined 500 and 350 cc Italian championship race after he had taunted Renzo Pasolini on the 350 cc Benelli in the early stages.

*   *   *

MV have made such a remarkable contribution to World Championship racing that it is hard to say which years were the most important. Their light-weight machinery in the days of Cecil Sandford and Carlo Ubbiali made enormous impact in the 1950s, capturing nine world titles in just five years against tough opposition. Until the arrival of Honda on the 350 cc scene, John Surtees raced against the clock and little else in this and the 500 cc class—and it is a tribute both to that rider's character and skill and also to Count Agusta's abiding devotion to the sport that there was so much thrilling racing and that records continued to fall. Hailwood and Agostini later continued the mastery.

However, perhaps the late 1960s and early '70s were the true heyday of MV, certainly in terms of results. The factory dominated both 500 and 350 cc classes with some of the finest racing machines ever produced and while some antipathy came their way because of their Goliath status, motor cycle racing gained much from their continued presence. It would have been easy for Count Agusta to withdraw along with the other Italian manufacturers in the late 1950s and even easier in the 1960s. Through his commitment to racing the boundaries of performance continued to extend, the full-blooded sound of those fabulous MV four-strokes continued to be heard among the high-pitched screams of the two-stroke take-over and racing continued to benefit in the public eye through factory participation and the glamour that only works entries and factory riders can command.

Their strong position in a strange way made them all the more vulnerable. The mere suggestion of defeat became a disaster and it was not long before the Japanese were taking them on. Thus came some of the most exciting years of World Championship racing since the modern series was started in 1949. Remember the sensational challenge of Yamaha in the 350 cc class through the enormous talent of Jarno Saarinen in 1971 and '72?

For the present, however, MV's problem continued to be Benelli. Having finished runner up to the MV in the 350 cc class in 1968, they were back in 1969 with new works machines (which had improved frames and engine torque) and a firm intention to contest a selected number of classic rounds. With less than a full-scale involvement in the championship they could hardly be seen as a serious threat to MV in the World Championships, but to score in just one or two rounds would give them sufficient honour and suggest that MV were perhaps not invincible after all. In early-season Italian races Pasolini was at his hectic best. On a drizzle-soaked circuit at Rimini in March, he fought a race-long duel with Agostini, with the edge always resting with the Benelli. Pasolini led from start to finish and in spite of a desperate effort by Agostini in the closing laps, was able to win with comfort.

Outpaced by the new race-fettled Benelli, the MV camp must have doubted their tactics in giving Agostini the 1968 350. Brand new six-cylinder machines which had been rumoured early in 1968 had finally emerged and Agostini had tested both 350 and 500 cc versions at Modena Autodrome during the week. Although the tests were said to have been successful, it was decided to play safe at Rimini and race the well-tried three-cylinder machines on which Agostini had been virtually unbeatable the previous year. The new MVs followed the basic Honda layout with the cylinders in line across the frame. There was a lot of interest in these new six-cylinder bikes, particularly since MV, remember, had built a six-cylinder transverse 500 in 1957 which John Hartle raced without success in the Italian Grand Prix. Although MV took Rimini's 500 cc race with ease, Benelli caused the excitement of the day as Pasolini won the 250 event to score a convincing double.

MV frowns deepened following the Riccione meeting a couple of weeks later. In an epic duel, Benelli and Pasolini proved they could be a serious contender for the 350 cc world title by once again beating Agostini on the MV fair and square. It was a wheel-to-wheel fight for several laps, much to the delight of the 40,000 crowd, and Pasolini went on to complete the 250 and 350 double. Meantime the MV mechanics admitted the defeat to be the worst that they had yet suffered against Benelli and as Agostini continued to ride the previous season's three-cylinder MV, they revealed that the new six-cylinder bikes were not yet considered sufficiently competitive.

In Spain at the opening round of the championships, the rivalry between the two camps exploded into outright conflict when Innocenzo Nardi-Dei, team manager of Benelli, withdrew works rider Pasolini from the 350 cc race in a shock move. He made an allegation of bad sportsmanship against Agostini and MV stating that when Benelli arrived at the Jarama circuit, being used for the first time for a classic round, Agostini was already practising although official training was not due to begin until the following day. When Pasolini asked to be allowed the same facility he was told that MV and Ossa had booked the exclusive use of the course and that he must ask them. The request was turned down and the Benelli team manager immediately withdrew saying that if Agostini wanted to practise alone he could also race alone. With the Benelli threat removed, MV took the honours in the 350 cc race from the Aermacchi of Kel Carruthers and made it a double with an easy win in the 500 cc event.

As in 1968, it turned out that there was nothing in grand prix racing to touch the mighty combination of MV and Agostini in 1969. The early season threat from Benelli and Pasolini in the 350 cc series did not develop and Agostini won the championship comfortably from Grassetti, who rode Yamaha and Jawa during the season. MV might well have had a more difficult passage but for the tragedy which cost the exciting Bill Ivy his life. After the diminutive rider's bitter feud with Phil Read when they were both Yamaha riders in 1968, Ivy had announced his retirement in a public expression of self-confessed disillusionment, declaring he never wanted to race again. However, the opportunity of a works contract with Jawa during 1969 rekindled old ambitions and he showed he meant business by riding second to Agostini at Hockenheim and Assen. Ivy seemed to be the only rider that season capable of offering any kind of challenge to Agostini in the 350 cc series and was reawakening us to the possibility of seeing MV being forced to fight hard for their premier position when tragedy struck and the talented rider was killed while practising for the East German Grand Prix at Sachsenring.

Diminutive Bill Ivy on the Jawa provided a strong challenge to Agostini and MV before his tragic crash in 1969. Bill is seen leading Agostini at the Dutch TT in 1968 (Mick Woollett).

In the 500 cc series Agostini and MV once again had a storming season. With 12 rounds that year, Agostini dominated every grand prix and although there was no need for him to appear at Imola and Opatija in the final two rounds, he finished the season with three times the number of points of his closest contender, Gyula Marsovszki, on a Linto machine. Curiously, it was this rider on the Linto who, in an early season burst, had destroyed a number of MV-held records.

In an astonishing catalogue of success the MV-Agostini partnership scored double 350/500 cc victories in Spain, West Germany, the Isle of Man, Holland, East Germany, Czechoslovakia, Finland and Belfast—a 100 per cent record. Still riding the well-tried three-cylinder MVs, Agostini scored his second TT double in two years to equal the achievement of only two other riders—racing's legendary Stanley Woods and John Surtees, the latter also on MV, of course. In the Senior race Agostini was not required to ride the remarkably reliable MV to its limit but, in spite of an absence of serious challengers, he raced with dedication and

took the machine to within one mile an hour of the winning average of 104.75 mph set two years before by Mike Hailwood in the fierce scrap he had on the Honda in the same race against Agostini. The success brought MV the distinction of winning the same number of solo TTs as the once incomparable Norton.

It was a coasting victory again in the Junior race with the MV totally in command and the superb three-cylinder machine in as good fettle at the end as when it started. There was some comment at the time that six laps for the Junior race was not enough—certainly an accurate observation about the MV.

Although MV and Agostini had taken some stick from racing fans who wanted to see more than a procession of easy wins, however impressive they may be, there were just as many who encouraged the Italian effort to keep factory support alive in racing. To these people the suggestion that the end of the road might now be in sight for the all-conquering combination came as a shock. The news broke at about TT time. If not common knowledge, no particular effort was made by the rider or the factory to hide the fact that Agostini's current contract with MV ran out at the end of the year, although everyone assumed that its renewal for 1970 was simply a technicality. Agostini had already enjoyed a few car races and had been offered a contract by Ferrari to drive in Formula 2 races in South America during the winter. It seemed the handsome Italian was on the way to following the example of John Surtees when he admitted: 'In 1970 I hope to race cars, but I may combine this with a few motor cycle races'.

In the meantime, Agostini crowned a remarkable season of success for himself and for MV by riding in six major end-of-season races at Mallory Park and Brands Hatch, winning five of them. At Mallory's International Race of the Year meeting in September the prospect of seeing Mike Hailwood, making what many believed would be his last appearance on a motor cycle, and Phil Read, as well as Agostini, attracted nearly 60,000 to the famous 1.35-mile Leicestershire track. In his best-ever performance on a British short circuit, the World Champion beat back his illustrious challengers to win all the three major races. A month later at Brands Hatch the all-powerful combination won the 500 cc Redex Trophy and the 20-lap *Evening News* major races with ease, though was beaten surprisingly into second place in the first race of the programme for 350s by Phil Read on the Yamaha. It was an exciting encounter, with Agostini holding Read back up to Westfield Bend on the first lap, but then Phil saw his opportunity and once in front did not give the MV a chance to get ahead again, though

Agostini hung on grimly until the machine lost its edge as Agostini forced it to the limit. There was ten seconds between the two riders at the finish.

The year, though phenomenally successful for MV on the race circuits, was less generous in another way for Count Mario Agusta, a younger brother of Count Domenico, the MV chief, had a heart attack and died at the end of September at only 53 years of age. He was a senior executive of the company and sometimes attended race meetings in Italy in which works MVs were competing.

For all the race success of MV in 1969, the major disappointment for the fans was the failure of the six-cylinder racers to emerge as a confident successor to the remarkable three-cylinder machines. The year virtually saw the end, certainly until his limited comeback in the TT Races of 1978, of the great Mike Hailwood. Disillusioned with Honda at the end of 1968 and having been denied the 500 cc World Championship by MV, Hailwood did not keep his interest in re-joining MV a secret. Before the Monza meeting towards the end of 1968, Mike said he had not received an actual offer from MV about riding for them in 1969, but team manager Arturo Magni confirmed that he had raised the possibility (presumably with Count Agusta) after Mike had said he would be interested. Mike admitted he had not been particularly happy since leaving MV at the end of 1966.

However, a firm offer from MV never came and Hailwood, now concerned to advance his racing career, moved into motor racing and Agostini, single handed, took MV to two more world titles in 1969.

Chapter 13

New chapters in racing history

MV and Agostini continued to be racing's 'dynamic duo' during 1970 and '71. In the 350 cc series they were faster and more reliable than the competition, though there were early rumblings during 1970 of Yamaha's forthcoming penetration. Riders like Kent Andersson and Rodney Gould were moving into higher placings as the season advanced, though it continued to be the Benelli machines of Kel Carruthers and Renzo Pasolini which were nearest to the MV in the early rounds. With an eye to the future—and with Agostini's self-declared ambitions in car racing—MV took an interest in a second rider to support Agostini in both classes. Angelo Bergamonti had tested works MVs at Modena and although at the time Count Agusta would not say what his plans were, the Italian rider's future seemed secure as he joined Agostini at

Monza. He ran second to the master there and took over as MV's number one in the last round in Spain which Agostini, already an easy World Champion, decided to miss. Once more MV claimed the most astonishing record, winning all 11 rounds in the 500 cc class and all ten in the 350 cc class.

At the end of 1970 MV's record was now beyond all comparison. For three complete seasons Agostini had won every 500 cc World Championship race he had contested and it stands to the monumental credit of the Italian factory in all departments that the outstanding reliability of the engine of the record-breaking MV had at the end of 1970 gone an unprecedented 30 races without serious mechanical breakdown.

Round the circuits the untouchable combination of Agostini and MV were writing whole new

In 1970 Giacomo Agostini rode to many lone victories on the 500 cc MV, including the Ulster Grand Prix, his tenth 500 cc grand prix race victory that year (B.R. Nicholls).

Supreme in Holland 1970—MV Agusta and Agostini going full blast (Mick Woollett).

chapters into the record books. A TT double in 1970 brought MV's tally of TT wins to 30, just four short of the all-time record of 34 held by Norton. It had taken Norton more than 50 years to achieve their record. MV's remarkable performance had been accomplished in just 18 years. Agostini was using the MV to build his personal reputation in a most dramatic way on the Isle of Man. In 1966 he had become the first Continental rider to win a Junior TT. Two years later he was the first Continental rider to score the coveted Senior-Junior double. Then in 1970 he became the first rider ever in the 63 years of TT racing to win the Senior and Junior TTs three years in succession.

There seemed to be nothing on the horizon which might even remotely offer the MV a serious challenge, yet the factory were not complacent about their position, particularly in the 350 cc class. The performance of the Benelli racer in earlier rounds had caused them some anxiety, but it was to MV's advantage that relations between Benelli and their star rider, Pasolini, were not developing satisfactorily and it came as no real surprise to the

Benelli camp when the talented, bespectacled Italian rider was given his marching orders. Benelli chiefs were convinced that they had a faster machine than MV and felt that, had Pasolini tried harder, they could have won more rounds.

Benelli, who were rumoured to have tried to tempt Agostini away from MV before with a contract worth more than £30,000 for a year, now made another approach to the World Champion, but Agostini decided to remain loyal to MV in spite of the Italian factory's signing of Bergamonti to a two year contract.

MV also had in their sights the fast-developing power of the ultra-fast Yamahas and to counter impending competition were anxious to develop a new 350. Their attempts with the six-cylinder 350 had not been a success and although that machine had been tested by Agostini way back in 1969 it had never been raced. Tests with a new machine had been due in November 1970 at Monza and reports suggested that it would be a V4, but it was not until the Monza meeting in September the following year that the new four-cylinder 350 had its first public showing. It was a disaster. Ridden by Alberto Pagani, on the factory MVs for the first time, the machine broke down on lap 5 and with Agostini also going out on the same lap on one of the factory's three-cylinder models, and retiring also in the 500 cc race, MV's only thin gleam of light came from Pagani's victory in the 500, though Agostini had raised the lap record to 127.09 mph before retiring.

Yamaha were to prove in 1971 that MV's concern had been well founded. In nine of the 11 rounds forming the 350 cc World Championship that year, Yamaha bikes ran second, with the brilliant Finnish rider Jarno Saarinen showing a lot of skill and winning in Czechoslovakia and Italy. He also took second place behind Agostini in Finland.

1971 started disastrously for MV. In February Count Domenico Agusta, the famous factory's equally famous founder, died following a heart attack and Bergamonti was fatally injured at Riccioni's pre-season international meeting, crashing while chasing Agostini in the 350 cc race.

He died in hospital at Bologna after having signed for MV only six months before. On the grand prix circuits, despite Saarinen's spirited challenge, Giacomo Agostini once more took MV through the 350 and 500 cc World Championships without serious trouble. With the 350 machine he won six races and registered eight wins in the 500 cc class. In doing so Agostini won his tenth world title. No rider had won more. Even Ubbiali and Hailwood, with nine each, had now been overtaken. For the one rider who was to remain with MV for almost the whole of his career, it was an astonishing record. In Agostini, Count Agusta had found the Italian rider who had made all his dreams come true.

Giacomo Agostini, now the undisputed giant of grand prix racing, had first ridden a motor cycle when he was 11 and was just 18 when he had his first race. In three years he was Italian champion. After riding for Morini he signed for Count Agusta and his illustrious career with MV began. His riding with MV made him a superstar and although he came from a wealthy Italian family, his racing

Agostini at Quarter Bridge on the Isle of Man, taking the MV three to victory in the 1971 Senior TT (B.R. Nicholls).

An unusual sight—Agostini and the MV in second place! He is led by Jack Findlay on a Suzuki in the 500 cc Belgian Grand Prix of 1971—which the conquering MV combination finally won (Mick Woollett).

successes made him a great deal richer. Born in 1943 at Lovere, near Bergamo in Northern Italy, his first outings were in domestic road races in Italy and in hill climb events. In 1963 he borrowed a Morini from the factory and entered his first major road race. A year later he became Morini's number one rider and won the 250 cc Italian championship from Tarquinio Provini. Shortly afterwards he was spotted by MV and Count Agusta signed him as number two rider to Mike Hailwood. In spite of his limited experience on a heavier machine he ended the season as runner up to Hailwood in the 500 cc World Championship. Motor cycle racing's most successful rider was on his way.

Agostini, the eldest of four brothers, became one of the most popular figures in racing. With his Latin good looks and carefree bachelor style, he enjoyed enormous box-office appeal over many years. Girls flocked around him wherever he raced and he enjoyed the respect of more serious race followers as well. He was in demand as a photographic model and appeared in a number of films. In the early 1970s Agostini was probably at his peak, riding MV

machines. He was really in a class of his own on the larger capacity machines. For most of his career Agostini was able to avoid the arguments and controversies which seemed to beset many of his contemporaries. There were few tempestuous scenes, no real feuds—though the back-biting with Hailwood was worth a few minor headlines. It was later, with his career past its peak, that he became more vehement as Phil Read, recruited by Count Agusta, stole his thunder by robbing him of the 500 cc title. After all those thrilling and successful years he finally split with Count Corrado Agusta though, to his credit, his fight back to take the world title one more time for Yamaha was an astonishing performance. British fans were devoted to the smiling, handsome Italian until he dug in his heels, slanged the Isle of Man TT Mountain Course and refused to race there after 1972 because he considered it too dangerous. It was that year that his friend, Gilberto Parlotti, was killed racing on the island and the tragedy distressed Agostini. He not only boycotted the Isle of Man thereafter, but led an active campaign to influence other top riders against competing there. He wanted the TT Races taken out of the World Championships and his strongly-expressed views, combined with the growing toll of casualties on the Isle of Man, certainly had some influence on the eventual decision to strip the TTs of their World Championship status.

Agostini's relationships with Count Domenico Agusta were largely cordial and his long association with MV was extremely happy and fruitful for them both. He had a deep respect for the factory and its founder. He said in 1968: 'I am proud to belong to MV because they have always given support to racing. This is because Count Agusta is an enthusiast and because it is his hobby rather than a business. It costs him a lot of money and though he does not go to many races, he knows what is happening'.

After the strong Honda challenge in the later 1960s, the MVs were not developed all that much. It was not really necessary. These superbly engineered and very reliable machines could win races comfortably just as they were. There was nothing to touch them. Never the fastest bikes available, they were superior because they handled better and could keep going against the pressure when other bikes packed in. MV in fact, for year upon year, preached one of the basic doctrines of motor cycle racing which those who challenged them either ignored or failed to understand: that speed and power, by themselves, are not enough. The machine has to be capable of handling well and of keeping going under pressure. When Kawasaki began moving into racing, Dave Simmonds, who led the grand prix assault, reckoned that the works 500 cc Kawasaki, on its day, was as fast as Agostini's MV. But reliability is as essential as outright speed.

What Agostini earned with MV has never been officially disclosed. He said more than once that MV were very generous, adding: 'But I have to do what they say'. He also made no secret of his particular liking for the three-cylinder MV. He joined the factory just as they were completing the first bike and he was the first to ride it. It was a small, low machine and it was understood that MV tailored it to Agostini's needs, following his experience on the 250 cc Morini. One of the surprising aspects of Agostini's meteoric rise to fame was that when Count Agusta recognised his potential and signed him for the grand prix circus, he had very little experience of riding outside Italy, though of course he had done exceptionally well in his own country. After Hailwood left MV, on his own admission, it was Agostini who gave him some of the hardest rides of his career, both in the 350 and 500 cc classes. Hailwood once assessed him as the finest Italian rider since Ubbiali, a quick learner with plenty of courage and skill.

Until his boycott of the island, Agostini had ridden there with tremendous success. Between 1966 and 1972 he won a total of ten TTs and on four occasions did the 'miracle' of winning the Junior and Senior races in the same year.

At the end of 1971, with Domenico Agusta dead, the question was: would MV continue racing? With domestic sales showing no signs of recovery as the mighty Japanese factories built up momentum, MV's racing policy must have been in the balance. Domenico had been succeeded in the business by the last and youngest of the Agusta brothers, Corrado, who had at one time shown interest in motor cycle racing.

However, for 25 years MV racing had been the inspiration of one man, Domenico, who alone had dictated the racing policy, decided what machines would be available, which riders would be offered contracts and which races MV would support. Once the driving force had gone the whole racing empire must have been in jeopardy.

As so often in the past, MV decided to continue racing at a time when it might have been easier to withdraw—and in 1972 they were set to face their strongest challenge yet from Yamaha.

Chapter 14

Saarinen and the Yamaha

If anything, 1972 put MV more surely in command of the 500 cc World Championship. Not only did Agostini retain the premier title to give the factory an unprecedented 15th successive championship in this class, but they also collected a second place through Alberto Pagani, who had been signed by MV towards the end of the previous season as second string to Agostini following the fatal crash of Bergamonti. So enormous was the gap between MV and any other challenger that Agostini's total of 105 points from the championship rounds was more than double the number amassed by third place occupant Bruno Kneubuhler of Switzerland on a Yamaha.

This was a fine performance by MV and Agostini, achieved in the face of a strong challenge from Yamaha. Already supreme in the 250 cc class, Yamaha had begun fiercely contesting the 350 cc category and to complete a fullblooded challenge provided a number of riders with specially enlarged 350 machines to make them eligible for racing in the 500 cc category.

In the 350 cc class MV and Agostini had their toughest year in a long time. Yamaha had brought a new competitiveness to top class racing and in their new sensation from Finland, Jarno Saarinen, they had discovered a rider who was not intimidated by Agostini's giant reputation. After serving notice following a number of impressive rides in 1971 while under contract to the Yamaha dealer in Finland, the blond racer whose brilliance was to shatter racing out of its complacency, had been given a works contract in 1972.

At first MV seemed reluctant to recognise the threat, despite Saarinen's excellent displays in 1971, and left Agostini with machines which were fundamentally the same as the previous year. In Germany and France, in the first and second rounds of the 350 cc championship, MV were left in no doubt that for the first time in years they had a king-sized fight on their hands. Saarinen's brilliant riding brought him victory in both races. MV now got the message. They signed Phil Read to give support to Agostini in the 350 cc class while Pagani was left to concentrate on the 500 cc races. They also introduced a new four-cylinder 350 machine. Rushed into service to stem the Yamaha advance, it was raced by Agostini for the first time at the

Austrian Grand Prix in May, after the demoralising defeats in West Germany and France by Jarno Saarinen. The new machine had a bore and stroke of 52 mm × 40.4 mm at a maximum 15,000 rpm. Weighing 308 lb, it had four valves per cylinder, twin camshaft, magneto ignition and a seven speed gearbox.

MV who, not without some surprise, had increased their racing budget a year before to combat the growing two-stroke menace, now had more riders and machines in the field than for years. Even so, Agostini had been beaten into second place in West Germany and was down to an almost unbelievable fourth position in France. Not for five years had the combined might of MV and Agostini been beaten so conclusively on equal terms. So devastating was Saarinen's win in West Germany

The 'Flying Finn' Jarno Saarinen who, on the works Yamaha, posed such a threat to MV and Agostini, with the Race of the Year trophy at Mallory Park in 1972 (J. Stoddart).

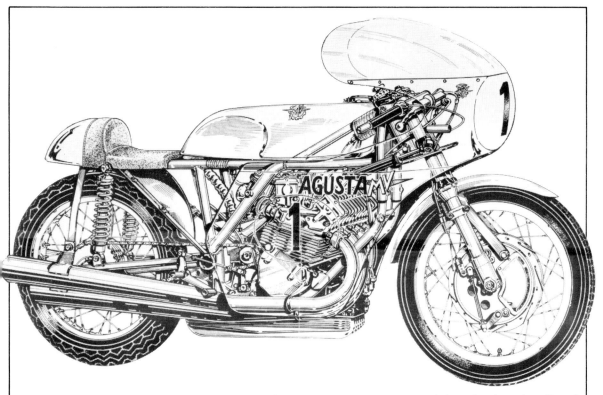

The four-cylinder 350 cc MV raced for the first time by Giacomo Agostini at the Austrian Grand Prix in May 1972, after being beaten in the first two grands prix in West Germany and France by Jarno Saarinen on the works Yamaha (Drawing by Bruce Smith courtesy of *Motor Cycle News*).

that he took the lead on the second lap and shattered the record three times before setting a new outright best for the circuit at 90.85 mph.

In Austria and Italy, MV fought back strongly and Agostini won both rounds, as he did in the Junior TT. For Agostini, the TT races of 1972 ended an era. He decided never to race there again following the tragic death of his close friend Gilberto Parlotti. For a while the entire MV team's continued presence on the island was in the balance. Pagani was grief-stricken at the fatal crash of his team mate, as was Agostini, and together with team manager Arturo Magni they discussed whether they should continue and race in the Senior event. There were frantic telephone calls to Italy for direct advice from headquarters, but the team was unable to make contact and had to take the decision themselves. Reports have suggested that the final decision was left to Agostini and, while the Senior TT was put off for $2\frac{1}{2}$ hours because of bad weather, the MV team pondered. Agostini decided in the end that they should go on and he won the Senior race, with Pagani second. It was MV's and Agostini's fifth consecutive Senior victory and the brilliant Italian had now set up the unique record of 53

racing laps of the TT course at more than 100 mph. Even so, for both MV and Agostini, the TTs had claimed one victim too many and they were never to return to race on the Isle of Man.

Agostini fought tenaciously for the 350 cc title, winning again in Holland. Phil Read on the other MV won in East Germany and, after Saarinen had brought the championship back to life again with a sensational win in Czechoslovakia, the Swedish round at Anderstorp was crucial. The racing was dramatic and tension-packed as Agostini roared round the $2\frac{1}{2}$-mile circuit in the lead. But the 'Flying Finn', as Saarinen was now tagged, had a World Championship in his sights and did not mean to surrender without a fight. For a while he kept close to the MV, but then the gearbox on the Yamaha began to give trouble. Saarinen lost ground—and all chance of winning the round. Agostini rode the MV majestically to win, Phil Read brought MV a second place and Saarinen finished third. Agostini won again in Finland to set the seal on MV's ninth World Championship in the 350 cc class, but it had been a closer-run battle than for years and Saarinen's runner-up tally of 89 points against the 105 points of Agostini suggested a much easier victory for MV than it had been in reality.

Saarinen was now the rider that everyone was talking about. He was the most exciting personality to emerge in racing, perhaps since Agostini himself. He was born in 1945 in the Finnish port of Turku and had raced on dirt and ice in Finland before moving into road racing. He became Finnish ice racing champion. His debut in road racing was elementary enough, when he rode a 125 cc Puch in 1967, to be followed by his own Yamaha in 1968. His first World Championship ride came in 1969, but he decided that he could not afford the finance of grand prix racing without a works contract and was about to abandon the blue riband sphere of motor cycle racing when his victory in the 350 cc Czechoslovakian Grand Prix of 1971 opened the door to an offer of works machines for 1972. He is down in the record books as 250 cc World Champion in 1972, nothing more, but this gives no reliable indication of his enormous talent and the impact he made on racing. Disastrously, early in 1973 he was not to survive the appalling tangle of wreckage following a multiple pile-up at Monza and the end came just as he was reaching the peak of his career.

In the short time that remained, Saarinen and Yamaha were to pose the biggest threat for more than a decade for MV and Agostini. Yamaha were moving into the premier position as a racing factory by this time. MV had long been a racing factory veteran when Yamaha collected their first world title through Bill Ivy in the 125 cc class in 1967. The following year Phil Read brought them the 125 and 250 cc World Championship double and after losing some ground in terms of results in 1969 and '70, they came back strongly again, through Read particularly, in 1971. However, Saarinen's colourful success had opened up a chink in MV's armour and Yamaha recognised the signs. With a little more effort and concentration they reckoned the 350 cc championship could now be theirs for the taking and, with excellent results in 1972 to build on and with Saarinen in spectacular form, 1973 looked like being a very lean year indeed for MV.

The racing Finn showed he meant business by winning brilliantly at Daytona and Imola and then made a sensational opening to the World Championships. In the 250 cc class, which held no interest of course for MV, he won the first three rounds in France, Austria and West Germany. This was good enough to put him well in the lead in the championship race, but in the 500 cc class Saarinen was writing even bigger headlines. While everything seemed to be going right for Saarinen and Yamaha,

the fortunes of Agostini and the MV flagged. MV gave the early season race at Imola a miss and at Mettet, in Belgium, although the Italian ace took the 'old' MV three to victory in both legs of the 500 cc event, his race speed was well below Saarinen's record average of 122.6 mph of the previous year.

Then in April, in the opening 500 cc World Championship round, Agostini could not keep the MV three in touch with the Finnish superstar. Before a record 65,000 crowd at the Paul Ricard circuit in the south of France, the searing pace of Saarinen on a new Yamaha four took him round the 3.6-mile circuit in 2 min 14.8 secs for a new absolute lap record. The pace proved too much for the MV three of Agostini, who crashed in a valiant but vain attempt to keep up with the Yamaha. The consolation for MV spelled a further threat to the, until now, secure position of Agostini as the premier 500 cc rider. For Phil Read, riding a new MV four kept the Italian factory in the picture to finish second.

In France Saarinen had ridden the new Yamaha four for the first time and after tempting Agostini into an all-out race for first place, easily convinced the MV camp that they were facing the biggest threat to their position at the top of 500 cc class racing since Mike Hailwood's Honda challenge of seven years before. In Austria, in the second round, Agostini had only managed to be third fastest in practice behind Saarinen and Kanaya, also on a Yamaha. After electrical trouble eliminated both Agostini and Read in the 350 cc race, Read appeared set to restore something of MV's flagging prestige as he moved off superbly in the 500 cc event and held on to the lead for two laps before Saarinen went ahead. Phil fought back tenaciously and on the high-speed Salzburgring, made treacherous by persistent drizzle, there was high drama for two more laps. On the 150 mph section Read got so close to Saarinen that the two machines touched and each rider condemned the other's tactics—Read claiming that Saarinen had cut into him in an effort to establish the best line for the corner, Saarinen saying that he had been compelled to brake hard to avoid Read forcing him into the straw bales. Meantime, Agostini never looked like getting in touch with the leaders on the MV three which was simply too slow. After only five laps he was all of 25 seconds behind Saarinen and more than nine seconds behind Kanaya in third place. Read's MV dropped a valve on the 17th lap and, as Saarinen went on to take the flag, the astonishing feature of the race was that no MVs finished the course. In the 500 cc championship table, after two rounds, Read was the highest placed MV rider, down in fifth place, while in the race for the 350 cc crown

Agostini was in joint third position with Janos Drapal (Yamaha).

At Hockenheim for the West German Grand Prix in May, MV did better in the 500 cc race, though earlier both their 350 cc bikes broke down with valve trouble and rumours spread quickly that they were considering pulling out of racing because of adverse results and publicity. However, a magnificent win by Read in the 500 cc race scotched the rumours.

In a bid to counter the Yamaha threat, MV had rushed through a bigger four-cylinder racer. The original version had a bore and stroke of 56 mm × 44 mm, a capacity of 432 cc and produced 80 bhp at 14,000. Yamaha had soon proved that it was not fast enough and MV set about producing a full-size 500 cc version. It was ready for the Hockenheim Grand Prix, flown to the circuit and fitted for the final practice session. Read, doing better in the championship than Agostini, was given the new machine, much to the Italian's disgust. The full-sized MV had a bore and stroke of 57 mm × 49 mm and gave 95 bhp at 14,000 rpm.

Phil rode a spectacular race tucking himself neatly behind Saarinen as they went into the first right-hander leading to the straight which takes the riders out of sight of the grandstand. As they came once more into view, Read was in the lead and he stayed there, in spite of constant pressure from Saarinen for more than 60 miles, to cross the line first. Saarinen was forced to retire after setting a new record lap when the rear chain on the Yamaha snapped. Read said afterwards that the new MV 500 cc four was faster on the straights than the Yamaha.

MV hopes rose for Monza, the next round, for team manager Arturo Magni had stayed away from Hockenheim in order to prepare a second new MV for Agostini. At the ill-fated Italian Grand Prix Agostini did his chances in the 350 cc championship race a power of good by grabbing maximum points in one of the toughest races of his career. There was a 100,000 home crowd which was bursting with speculation following a report in an Italian newspaper the day before that Agostini would shortly be leaving MV for Honda (later denied by Agostini). The Italian ace was harried first by team mate Read, then by Teuvo Lansivuori and finally by Renzo Pasolini on a Harley-Davidson which was quicker than Agostini's machine. The World Champion admitted: 'I was a little lucky to win', but with four 350 cc rounds now gone, Agostini had hoisted himself into second place behind Lansivuori and was just seven points in arrears.

Then, at the start of the 250 cc race, came the appalling 15-machine pile-up which claimed the lives of Saarinen and Pasolini. The 500 cc event, in which MV were tipped as having a good chance of winning, was struck from the programme.

As Yamaha now faced a desperate situation, MV Agusta had time to reflect on the severe problems which had beset them since before the beginning of the year. Labour unrest in the Italian motor cycle industry had cost the factory hundreds of valuable working hours over a period of some five months and had made it impossible to complete on schedule the new 350 cc and 500 cc machines which everyone, including Count Corrado Agusta, recognised as essential if MV were to counter the fierce competition from Yamaha. As a result of this, MV had been forced to suspend official support for grand prix racing at the start of the season, giving their sanction to Agostini and Read to race the 1972 machines under a private arrangement. After the poor showing of the MVs at Modena, Roki Agusta, son of the Count and now involving himself with the firm's racing effort, had said it was important to throw all their effort into the World Championships, even if it meant sacrificing their anticipated programme of Formula 750 races.

A further threat also seemed likely from Suzuki, who were set to launch an attack in the 500 cc class as MV struggled desperately to complete work on their new machines. In March they reckoned the 500 cc fours were nearing completion but were less hopeful about the new 350s. Arturo Magni revealed MV's dismal prospects at the start of 1973 when he said: 'We shall allow last year's machines to be raced as private entries, but if they prove not competitive after three or four grands prix and the new machines are not ready, it could be a good idea to pull out of racing for the rest of the season'.

The new 500 fours had their first circuit tests in March but, although Phil Read raced one of the new engines to second place in France, the MV team were clearly troubled after a series of engine tests and rushed a top engineer from their helicopter department into the race shop in an effort to sort out the problems. Though the new engine was undoubtedly faster, there was a question of reliability to be sorted out, but as Phil Read brought the new machine its first win at Hockenheim, it looked as though MV were perhaps back in business.

The death of Saarinen, who was at that time leading both 250 cc and 500 cc championships, eliminated MV's major threat to the retention of the 500 cc world title, for Yamaha withdrew their team as a mark of respect to Saarinen. Though Phil Read was now the major challenger, MV kept faith with their principles on safety at circuits and refused to

Agostini in action before British crowds at Mallory Park in 1973 (Mick Woollett).

go to the Isle of Man. Australian Jack Findlay on a Suzuki took the Senior race. Later that month MV did nothing to further their championship hopes when they boycotted the Yugoslavian Grand Prix at Opatija. They arrived to find that safety precautions were not what they expected and after inspecting the circuit went back home again. They had warned organisers earlier in the season that they would withdraw where they found race safety inadequate and had already threatened the organisers at the sea-front circuit that, unless major improvements were made on previous safety cover, they would not race.

Fortunately for MV, the winners on the Isle of Man and in Yugoslavia (Findlay and Ken Newcombe) were not to make any lasting impression on the championship that year, but Agostini was experiencing his worst season since he first became a superstar. With five races already held, plus the Monza meeting which, because of the multiple crash in the 250 cc class had been cancelled, Agostini had not won one 500 cc race; indeed he had not even scored one point in that class. Meantime, Phil Read was rapidly becoming MV's new wonder boy. He had run second to Saarinen in France and

had won in West Germany. His prospects began to look really good as he won in Holland, while Agostini was again unplaced, though the Italian won the 350 cc race and established a new lap record of 93.92 mph.

Desperately trying to regain his old form, Agostini's luck changed in Belgium and on the fast open sweeps of the famous Francorchamps circuit he raced to his first 500 cc victory of the season, ahead of Phil Read. It was an impressive ride as Agostini swept to a new race record at 128.43 mph and a new lap record at 130.85 mph. Read was not in the picture. After the MV mechanics had found two damaged pistons on his race machine only hours before the start of the race, Phil had to be content to maintain second place on the practice bike. All was still not well with the World Champion, however, for on a brief visit to Britain for races at Silverstone, he suffered a psychological defeat when he was convincingly beaten in the 500 cc race by both Phil Read and Barry Sheene.

Although Saarinen's death had removed the Yamaha challenge, MV had seen enough to realise they needed to do something to improve their machinery if they were to stay at the top in the premier class. At Misano in Italy, in August, Agostini tested a new four-cylinder 500 machine during practice for the big race and it showed sufficient potential for reports to emerge from within the MV camp that it would probably have its first major outing later in the season. The new bike was only a little bigger than the 350 cc MV and some 20 lb lighter than the MV four which Read had taken to victory at Silverstone. A report from Italy said that the engine size had been drastically reduced allowing the frame to be little bigger than the one used for the 350 engine. The fork angle had been altered and other slight modifications were apparent near the engine mountings.

The remaining four rounds saw a gigantic fight for the championship. MV were virtually home and dry once more and all that remained now was the decision as to which rider, Agostini or Read, would take the title. Although the two were team mates, open hostility broke out towards the end of the year as Agostini complained about Phil's boastful attitude. There is no doubt that at the start of the season Agostini had been the factory's number one rider but, as Read had begun to succeed and Agostini had struggled against poor form, the factory's emphasis had switched. As they saw Read in the better position to retain for them the coveted 500 cc title, they began to direct their attention to him. Agostini complained: 'My contract with MV Agusta ends in October. Before I sign a new one I intend to speak to Count Corrado Agusta and to clear some matters with Read, to whom I have given so much this year—even to the point of leaving myself with just one bike to defend the 500 cc title. Instead of being grateful, he has stolen some important victories from me'.

Perhaps there was some justification in what the Italian said. Read was never slow to recognise a good opportunity or pass over the main chance and his more successful riding of the MVs in 1973 gave him the opportunity to press his claim in the right quarters to become the factory's number one rider in 1974. On the other hand, Agostini's reaction was understandably tempered by his lack of success after being so long at the top and by the fact that, although there was still a great deal of superb racing left in the small, dynamic, handsome Italian, he was older than Phil and perhaps beginning to feel the insistent pressure of Read a burden.

Even so, it was Agostini's day in Czechoslovakia at the Brno circuit, with Read running home in second place, but the positions were reversed in Sweden. Agostini won again in Finland but the championship had already been decided and Phil

The 500 cc version of the MV three which dominated grand prix racing from 1968 to 1972 (D. Morley).

Read underlined his superiority during the year with a win in the final round in Spain.

Agostini's black season continued in September when he crashed in practice at Misano, near Riccione, badly injuring his left leg on the new lightweight 500 four. In Britain, the keenly anticipated clash between Agostini and Read had the additional flavour of the 'aggravation' which had developed during the season between the two riders, but it turned out to be the race that never was—for Agostini was forced to quit because of the pain in his injured leg.

It was a rueful, discontented Agostini who at the end of 1973 demanded special treatment from MV if he was to continue with the famous factory for 1974. He told Count Corrado Agusta that he wanted four works machines for his exclusive use, two for the 350 class and two more for the 500 cc class. After so many years, the champion, Agostini, had come to accept the 500 cc world title as his own and he was determined to recover his position in 1974. Read, on the other hand, had deliberately gone after a place in the MV team in a calculating way and said that MV had signed him on because they knew he was able to go as hard as they wanted him to. 'They wanted a winner even if it was team orders that Agostini should be first home', he said.

After Agostini had been soundly beaten by Saarinen at Clermont Ferrand in the 350 cc event in 1972, Read had made his overtures to MV, saying he felt he may be able to help Agostini in the fight against Saarinen and Yamaha. He was invited to Italy to meet Corrado Agusta and he said afterwards: 'There was no haggling, no trouble about cash. They said they would like me to ride the 350 and there was no doubt in my mind about turning down the offer. I made sure I was adequately compensated for the money I would lose by not riding in the 250 cc class'.

Read said that one of the reasons for switching to MV was the additional bait of a possible outing or two on the 500, which he described as the most exciting racing machine of all time. He admitted that his orders were to stay close to Agostini and claimed he could not really do otherwise because Agostini, as an Italian, was given whichever was the quicker machine and he (Read) had no real say in the choice because he could not speak Italian, so was in the hands of the MV mechanics. But Agostini was telling a different story!

In assessing Agostini, Read once said: 'He's an absolute superstar. Nobody can really work with him. Being Italian he is flamboyant and he likes to be number one. He works with that aim in mind. That is the only place for him. He is not very forthcoming and you do not get much out of him. At least, I didn't. In fact he is a bit off-hand'.

The relationship was anything but harmonious and for 1974 the unbelievable happened: after nine long years, during which time he had personified the company's racing success, Giacomo Agostini packed his bags and left MV. In December Phil Read had gone to Italy and signed a contract for 1974 to be MV's number one rider, while Agostini remained undecided about his future plans. Then, just before Easter, Agostini signed for Yamaha in spite of a dramatic bid for his signature by Honda. Giacomo Agostini was by then the most successful motor cycle racer of all time having won for MV six 350 and six 500 cc world titles in the space of just seven years.

Now the era had ended but the bitter battle between Read and Agostini, Yamaha and MV, was to continue for two more years. Then MV were themselves finally to disappear from the racing circuits of the world.

Chapter 15

The MV-Yamaha racing duel

By 1974 the balance of power in the larger capacity classes of the World Championships was beginning to change. Yamaha had been courageous enough in the previous two seasons to start knocking hard on MV's door, but it was to be their Japanese contemporary, Suzuki, who were to become the more powerful 500 cc contender in grand prix racing in the next few years.

Despite MV's continued interest in racing, times were undoubtedly changing at Gallarate. By the end of 1973 the Italian Government, whose interest had been based on MV's helicopter business, had secured a 51 per cent controlling interest in the company, though the factory stressed that this would not affect the race programme. The question was asked, however: is it the beginning of the end for MV? Weekly production of motor cycles, which was only ever a minimal part of the overall Agusta business, was by now down to about 50 or 60 (from a peak of nearly 200) with a labour force of about 1,000. Now that the Italian Government was taking more than just a financial interest, Count Corrado Agusta would find it increasingly difficult to justify an expenditure on racing which exceeded the profits made from motor cycle sales.

There seemed no doubt that MV wanted to go on racing, the Count seeing success on the circuit as a means of boosting motor cycle output, but whether the financial structure of the company could continue to permit racing was another matter. The answer in the long term might well rest with Corrado's willingness to foot the bill as a private venture.

For the moment, however, MV were to continue racing and an MV presence without Agostini, after all those years of absolute success, would seem strange indeed. After Agostini's departure to Yamaha (at a reputed £100,000 for the two year contract) MV possessed a team which consisted solely of Phil Read. Read himself, though younger than Agostini, was still something of a veteran so MV had not lapsed Agostini's contract because of a new 'youth' policy. While Phil Read might have accepted the idea of having Agostini as a team mate for another year, as World Champion it would have had to be on his terms, which meant that Agostini would have been forced to ride as number two. That situation, even with the temptation of a fat

contract, would have been intolerable for Agostini. So to that extent, the parting of the ways was inevitable. Agostini now regarded the 500 cc crown as his personal property and saw in the fast-developing Yamaha factory, with their immense resources based on commercial success, the best chance of regaining his 500 cc title. His move to Yamaha was, none the less, one of the most surprising in racing history. As the giants took up their battle stations for the new season, there was a more exciting, close-fought season in prospect than for years.

Though some would disagree, Read perhaps, on paper, started out favourite with the MV. He had the experience of a year's riding on the celebrated four-stroke while Agostini would not find it easy riding the two-stroke Yamaha after a career spent on four-strokes.

MV were taking no chances. Though it was by now certain that they were not the all-conquering power they had been under Count Domenico Agusta in the 1960s, they were still holding grimly to the few strong threads which attached them to racing. So they set about sorting themselves out for 1974. For a while it seemed that they would depend solely on Phil Read, but then Read suggested that Dieter Braun, the West German ace, might be just the rider to provide the support he required. Braun, who had captured the 250 cc world title in 1973 on a standard Yamaha, was not too sure about the prospects, for it was known that MV liked to have an Italian rider in their team because of the importance they attached to the Italian championships in which only Italian riders could race.

Meantime, Agostini was busy visiting the Yamaha headquarters in Japan, where he signed his two-year contract, and later returned to test-ride 350, 500 and 750 cc racers. Read was in Italy setting up his bikes for the new season and testing a four-cylinder 750 cc MV.

In February came the news that Braun was having second thoughts about the MV possibility. After Read had arranged for him to meet Count Corrado Agusta at the Swiss resort of St Moritz he said he was too ill to travel to Italy for test rides on the works MV and then admitted that he was concerned that with MV he would have only the 500 cc machine to ride, plus the possibility of the 350.

When Yamaha's European team manager Rodney Gould came up with an improved offer of cash support and made bikes available to Braun in the 250, 350, 500 and 750 cc classes, it appeared almost certain that the West German would turn down MV's offer. That supposition was indirectly confirmed two weeks later when, in a surprise move, MV Agusta signed the 28 year old Italian Gianfranco Bonera. After a dispute over a contract the promising Italian rider had quit Harley-Davidson and was about to buy a couple of racing Yamahas when Count Agusta came up with the offer. It shows just how quickly fortunes can alter in racing. A couple of years before there would have been a queue of riders scrambling to sign an MV contract. Now, with the powerful forces of Yamaha and Suzuki showing themselves to be the brighter prospects for the future, MV found themselves hard pressed when they went shopping for someone to support Phil Read. They first wanted Bonera, but the Italian had a Harley-Davidson contract, or so it appeared. Then Barry Sheene took their notice, but he had already signed for Suzuki. Dieter Braun was their third choice, but he rejected the offer. Then Bonera found he was not contracted to Harley-Davidson after all and MV stepped in quickly.

In the psychological battle which preceeds every grand prix season, the balance tipped first MV's way and then towards Yamaha. Read was early favourite for the 500 cc title, on which in 1974 he was to concentrate, as most observers contemplated the difficulties Agostini might face in adapting to the Yamaha two-strokes. However, as an injury to Read's finger sustained in a crash in 1972 continued to be troublesome, even after treatment and a couple of operations which were supposed to put it right, the critics began to favour Agostini. Responsible for the switch of opinion were Agostini's two sensational victories, at Daytona and Imola. There was some consolation for MV at Misano in March when, in the first pre-season clash between MV and Yamaha, Read came out on top as Agostini had to pull out of both the 350 and 500 cc races. Both factories had their problems prior to this important Italian meeting. Agostini's 500 cc Yamaha engine had 'blown up' badly in final practice and mechanics had to work through the night to repair it. MV, meantime, had been forced to smuggle their machines out of the factory because of a strike there and had to prepare them in a private workshop.

Something of the keen and, on the surface, good natured, rivalry which existed between Agostini and Read, MV and Yamaha, can be judged from Read's opportunist gamesmanship during practice.

Bonera making an impressive debut on the 500 MV at Mallory Park in 1974 (B.R. Nicholls).

Well in the lead at the Dutch TT of 1974. Behind Phil Read on the MV are Lansivuori (Yamaha), Bonera (MV), and on the other Yamaha, Agostini (Mick Woollett).

He dashed from the pits to help push Agostini's Yamaha into life, saying that as the Italian had no experience of two-stroke riding, he felt he ought to give him a helping hand! Behind the scenes, MV were still concerned about the lack of strength in depth of their team and even went so far as tentatively to approach the American ace, Gary Nixon, after the latter had crashed at Daytona when chasing the eventual winner Agostini.

Then it was curtain-up on the World Championships and immediately, in the 500 cc class, first honours went to MV. In France, at Clermont Ferrand, Read crossed the line first with that promised Suzuki challenge coming through as Barry Sheene took second place. Bonera was third on the second MV. Tension was high at the start. Phil Read knew the circuit well and was traditionally successful there. He underlined his intention with an impressive practice lap which equalled the seven-year-old absolute record of Mike Hailwood on a 250 cc Honda six in 1968. A record crowd of almost 100,000 saw Agostini move away to a poor start, but soon he was in flying pursuit of Read, who was leading the field. He shot into the lead and was

holding a nine-second advantage over the MV of Read when a gearbox bearing on Agostini's Yamaha smashed and he was out of the race, but not before setting a new absolute track record of 3 mins 32.4 secs, 3.6 secs ahead of Hailwood's previous best.

A strong challenge to the winning MV came from Barry Sheene on the Suzuki in the latter stages. Not until his pit signalled that Bonera was closing on him did he make his effort. Had he done so earlier he might even have overtaken the MV.

The second round at the Nürburgring was a shambles and can be discounted as a serious grand prix race because most of the top riders, including both the MV and Yamaha teams, in dispute with the German organisers over safety precautions at the circuit, refused to ride. However, in Austria, in the third round, Agostini stormed ahead once more to gain a pulsating 350/500 cc double victory with a maximum 15 points from each race. It was left to Bonera to save MV from humiliation with a fine ride to gain second place in the 500 cc race. He pushed Agostini hard for the entire race and was less than a quarter of a second in arrears when the

Yamaha crossed the line to win. It was a fine display by the young Italian who, at the time, had ridden in fewer road races in his entire career than Agostini was normally used to getting through in just one season. He might have done even better, but he misjudged his final challenge, not allowing sufficient time to weave through the tail-enders. Read, on the other MV, was never really in the running. The engine tightened and, after eight laps, finally seized.

With this excellent display, Bonera had heightened considerably MV's chances in the 500 cc class. With three of the ten races in the championship programme already over, he now led the championship jointly with Barry Sheene, whose 12 points in France and ten points in Austria, gave him a total of 22 points. Agostini, Read and Edmund Czihak were all on 15 points; the latter as a result of the West German debacle when all the stars had withdrawn.

In the 350 cc class, MV's prospects were grim. Agostini was well in the lead with 30 points, while the MVs had not yet collected a single point. Read had done well in France until the MV began to misfire which led to his withdrawal, and in Austria, after initially taking command, water in the ignition

Read astride a prototype 500 cc MV in practice for the Belgian Grand Prix of 1974. MV won the race for the 17th year in succession (Mick Woollett).

again put him out of the race.

As the grand prix circus took time off to contest the important Italian international meeting at Misano, Count Corrado Agusta made a sensational decision. With his riders and machines at the circuit, he telephoned the team and banned them from taking part in the 350 cc event. This shock move took the team by surprise, particularly in view of Bonera's performance on the 350 in practice when, for the first time since joining the factory, he had set the fastest time. The ban was effectively the withdrawal of MV Agusta from 350 cc racing, so the dismal retirement of Read in Austria was a disappointing and inappropriate end after the company had contributed so much to the class over so many years. Further humiliating (by MV standards) defeats seemed on the cards had Count Agusta not stepped in. He recognised a lost cause and concentrated his forces in retaining what was, after all, the more important and prestigious 500 cc crown. So for the first time in some 18 years, the familiar full-throated sound of the once all-conquering 350 MV was absent from the grand prix scene.

Now they set about the not inconsiderable task of winning that 500 cc title. Italy was a good round, with Bonera once again proving his worth with a fine win. Read was third and Agostini was unplaced. In practice Agostini on the Yamaha looked the master with the fastest lap, with Bonera and Read fractionally slower. Then came Lansivuori, Sheene and Jack Findlay. In the race itself, the Yamaha of Agostini was supreme, but after shattering the absolute lap record for the circuit, the Yamaha unbelievably ran out of petrol with two laps to go. Bonera raced on to record his first grand prix victory after just three classic outings on the works MV four. MV stuck to their principles once again by boycotting the Isle of Man, but in Holland, immediately afterwards, MV's hopes sustained a shattering setback when Agostini scored a fine win, with Read and Bonera finishing third and fourth. Agostini rode the Yamaha brilliantly to become the first man to lap the 4.78-mile Assen circuit in under three minutes. Everything seemed to go right for the Yamaha ace, while both Read and Bonera struggled with the handling of the MVs, not helped by a front brake fault. Read was almost 30 seconds behind Agostini at the end.

Sensing perhaps that something special was needed, Phil Read approached the Belgian Grand Prix at a crucial stage in the series. Collectively, MV were in a strong position, having Bonera with 45 points and Read with 35. Agostini's total stood at

30 points, but too close for MV comfort was Lansivuori's 32 points, while Barry Sheene with 22 could not be ignored. With 15 points available for a win it did not take long in championship racing for fortunes to switch dramatically. In any case, Read was personally interested in retaining the title for himself and would be less than 100 per cent happy if Bonera were to secure the title for MV. For the 35-year-old British World Champion, everything seemed to come together in Belgium. On the world's fastest grand prix circuit and with the MV going beautifully, he destroyed the Yamaha challenge with an astonishing performance. Reaching speeds around the 180 mph mark on the MV four, he shattered the lap record for the famous Spa circuit on every lap, finishing with a new record of 133.34 mph.

Yamaha had unveiled a new slimline four-cylinder 500 in practice and in an effort to counter the new threat, MV added aerofoils and enclosed rear-end fairings to their machines. These were discarded for the race, though Agostini elected to ride the new Yamaha. Read was already eight seconds ahead of Sheene, Agostini and Bonera in that order after only one lap. His first lap, from a standing start, produced an incredible 130.25 mph and by the end of the second lap he had increased his lead to 13 seconds. Riding one of the most convincing races of his career, Read not only set up a new lap record, but his new average race record of 131.90 mph was faster than the old lap record! It was a joyful occasion for the MV camp and exactly the morale booster the factory needed: Read's magnificent win hoisted him to the top of the 500 cc championship table for the first time since the opening round in France. Bonera, who collected only a single point in Belgium, was now four points behind his team mate, while Agostini, who had taken the Yamaha into a very worthwhile second place to gain 12 championship points, was now only four points in arrears and eight points behind Read.

Read's Francorchamps victory had maintained another phenomenal MV record, for now, at the Belgian circuit, they had not lost a 500 cc World Championship race for 17 years! It was really a sensational achievement. Read said after his superb win that the MV was set up correctly for Francorchamps and the brakes, handling and gearing were spot on. He predicted: 'If my machine is set up in the same way to deal with the Anderstorp circuit, I could win again in the next round in Sweden'.

If Belgium was right for Read and the MV, Anderstorp was just as unsuitable. During the whole of practice the MV riders somehow could not get the bikes to handle properly, but in the race itself the poor performance of the MVs did not count for too much. Barry Sheene crashed at the 120 mph sweeping right-hander at the end of the long straight. The MVs were able to avoid both Sheene and his Suzuki, but Agostini was less fortunate and his evading line took him into the crash fences and he came down heavily. Read and Bonera finished in second and fourth places. Agostini damaged a shoulder in the crash and was unable to ride in Finland. With two rounds remaining, it was now MV all the way, with Read and Bonera coming first and second in Finland and Czechoslovakia. Read's victory in Finland settled the championship in his and MV's favour, leaving the second place to be settled in the final round in Czechoslovakia, Bonera and Lansivuori in contention. Bonera set up a new record lap of 103.89 mph for the Brno circuit, eclipsing the old Hailwood/Honda record of 1967, and made sure of second place.

While MV's withdrawal from the 350 cc series after so many years of support was tinged with sorrow, their magnificent display in the 500 cc category had done much to compensate for it. Against the considerable combined strength of Agostini and Yamaha they had even improved on their performance of the previous season, in 1974 gaining first and second positions in the championship. While Agostini was unlucky to sustain an injury, the magnitude of the MV/Read victory was obvious. Bonera's performance, in his first grand prix season, was little short of phenomenal. Agostini, in the end, finished fourth.

Read's championship winning MV thorough-bred deserves some detailed mention. It had a bore and stroke of 57 mm × 49 mm and put out 95 bhp at 14,000 rpm. The cylinders, cast in one block, had separate steel liners and the pent-roof shaped combustion chamber had four valves per cylinder, actuated by twin camshafts, which were gear-driven from the middle of the crankshaft. The crankshaft itself was made up of five pieces pressed together with the crankpins set at 180 degrees.

Motor Cycle put the bike under the microscope at the time and reported: 'When the crankshaft is pressed up, ten roller bearings are involved—the four big ends plus six supporting the crankshaft.

'Drive to the American-built magneto, which juts out the front of the engine in a rather exposed position, is taken from the camshaft drive gear-train.

'Why, in these days of transistor and other trick ignition systems, do MV still stick to the good old-fashioned magneto? Simply because they have yet to test another system that is better.

'The oil-pump is driven from the clutch-drum but this only supplies oil to the camshaft drive gears. All the roller bearings on the crankshaft are lubricated by oil mist—and so is the six-speed gearbox.

'The under-engine sump oil-tank holds just under six pints—and to keep oil temperature down, an oil cooling radiator is mounted in the nose of the streamlining, with holes drilled through the number-plate to let the air through to the cooler.

'The 30 mm Dell'Orto carburettors, without fancy bellmouths and with separate float-chambers (one to each pair of carburettors) have a curiously dated look—but, like the magnetos, MV consider them the best available.

'The top half of the crankcase is in one with the cylinder block—and this bolts on to the lower half, of magnesium alloy, which includes the gearbox compartment and sump.

'Primary drive is by gears from the middle of the crankshaft to a countershaft. Every effort has been made to make the engine as light and as narrow as possible—and MV claim a weight of 121 lb and a width of just 16 inches.

'Finning of the cylinder block is interrupted— MV find that this helps to keep distortion to a minimum.

'The engine is hung in a chrome-moly frame with no tubes running under the engine. MV prefer this layout because it allows them to mount the unit as low as possible—and getting the weight low aids stability under racing conditions.

'Front forks are Ceriani. A special feature is that damping can be stiffened by turning an adjuster at the top of each leg. Movement totals four inches.

'Handlebars, levers and throttle are all made by MV themselves—and a quarter turn of the rider's right hand is sufficient to fully open the four throttles.

'Like the magneto and the carburettors, the rev counter has a slightly vintage look. Driven from the exhaust camshaft, it is a purely mechanical one— abandoned by most teams many years ago in favour of electrical types.

'Fuel tank capacity varies from a four gallon tank for the shorter races to six gallons for the longest grands prix—and fuel consumption never drops below 20 mpg, even on the thirstiest circuits.

'The rear fork is fabricated with strong box sections. Rear suspension units are Ceriani with nearly five inches of movement and, like the front forks, the damping is adjustable.

'American Morris magnesium alloy wheels are preferred, fitted with disc brakes—two ten-inch discs on the front and one nine-inch on the rear. The discs themselves are chrome plated light alloy with the friction surfaces sprayed with a special metallic compound.

'Tyres are British Dunlops, though Bonera tried the rival Michelin covers a time or two last season. And although the Morris wheels mean that they could be run tubeless, MV so far have preferred to err on the safe side and fit tubes, despite the extra weight.'

Despite the scares and the hiccups, MV Agusta had once again had a remarkably successful season, for although they had by now assumed the status of a colossus in racing, it must be remembered, in fairness to their achievement in 1974, that compared with Yamaha or even Suzuki at that time, MV was a very much smaller organisation, with fewer resources and with nothing like the kind of investment that the Japanese were prepared to put behind their racing ambitions.

Sadly, time was overtaking both MV Agusta and their remarkable racing machines, and 1974 was the last time they won a World Championship, in spite of the further confrontation with Yamaha in 1975. So it is perhaps opportune to look a little deeper at the careers of the two riders who rode what turned out to be MV's swansong in World Championship racing.

Phil Read and Gianfranco Bonera were very different personalities, but they combined in a formidable team to succeed in this last significant MV season. Philip William Read was born in Luton in 1939 and became one of Britain's most successful racers. His mother and father were motor cycle enthusiasts and Phil cut his teeth on the sight and sound of bike racing at Silverstone in company with his father. His first machine was a 250 cc side-valve Matchless which he bought when he was only 13. He first raced at Mallory Park in 1956 and won for the first time at Castle Combe the following year. He won a TT at his first attempt in 1961. His first grand prix victory came in France in 1964.

Read scored his first successes on Nortons in the early 1960s and was a member of the Geoff Duke Gilera come-back team in 1963. He gained his early international reputation riding the very quick Yamaha two-strokes and in a phenomenal five year spell brought the Japanese factory four World Championships. In 1971 he became the world's most successful 250 cc racer, having recorded since the beginning 25 wins in the class and a personal tally of 36 grand prix wins. For most of his career Phil Read has been a controversial character. Outspoken and strong willed, he grabbed the headlines in the 1960s through his feud with Yamaha team mate Bill Ivy, when he disobeyed team orders because the opportunity came for him to win a double World Championship. But his ability on a bike has never been in doubt and some of his 1960s victories for Yamaha were achieved against the most formidable opposition, including riders like Mike Hailwood and Jim Redman. He showed his versatility when, after exploiting all that the two-strokes had to offer in the middle classes— and into the bargain gaining four World Championships in eight years in the 250 cc class and the 125 cc World Championship in 1968 (when he was double World Champion)—he switched back successfully to four-strokes and took MV to victory in 1973 and '74.

Gianfranco Bonera was born in Monza, Italy, in 1946 and made his racing debut on a 125 cc Aermacchi in 1971, finishing fourth that year in the Italian junior 125 cc championships. In 1972 he was Italian junior champion in the 500 cc class. He made his grand prix debut in 1973 as one of the first private owners of the new 350 cc air-cooled, two-stroke, twin-cylinder racing Harleys, finishing third in the Yugoslavian Grand Prix. After a fourth position on the same machine in the Czechoslovakian Grand Prix that same year, Harley-Davidson seemed set to sign him to a full-scale works contract for 1974, but nothing materialised and he was prepared to buy himself a couple of racing Yamahas for 1974 when he got the chance to join MV. Before turning to motor cycle racing, Franco Bonera was a cycle champion, a heavy crash in 1968 bringing his career to an end. Three years later he decided to go racing again, but this time on motor cycles. A modest character, one of Franco's special skills was the ability to learn a race circuit extremely quickly. He was to be dropped by MV at the end of 1975 when he was signed by Harley-Davidson.

Chapter 16

A few more road models

Subsequent development of MV's road-going machines brought a marked improvement with appearance and colour reminiscent of the factory racers, along with a more powerful 750 cc version of the double overhead camshaft engine. This new machine had been on the market in Italy for close on three years when Gus Kuhn of London started importation in November 1972. A development of the original model caused a sensation when the brand new bike, similar in specification to the machine which Giacomo Agostini was scheduled to race at Daytona and on British short circuits in 1972, was unveiled at the Milan Motor Cycle Show in November 1971. Known as the 750 cc 'Super Sport', it produced 78 bhp and the factory claimed a top speed of 160 mph! The news from MV was that the 'Super Sport' would go into full production as a road machine in April to sell, in Italy, for about £1,600 including a racing style fairing. Shaft drive, with a much lighter frame than any earlier production line MVs and improved Ceriani brakes,

were included in the specification. Introduced at the same time was the 750 cc GT model—a four-cylinder machine of conventional design, but intended for the touring rider looking for top performance. A four-stroke scrambler—never really destined to reach the high spots against the much more competitive two-strokes—was also introduced at the Milan Show that year.

At Milan the following year, 1973, MV put on display a 350 cc four-stroke twin, a modern looking machine which the factory admitted was a prototype but which would go into production in 1974. It was designed by Giorgio Giugiaro, who had also produced the latest Ducatis and the Suzuki Wankel, and although no performance figures were given, the machine was of low, clean design and had magnesium wheels and twin disc front brake. It was an isolated MV flag-waver at Milan, for the remainder of their display consisted of rather tired-looking 350 cc sport and standard roadsters, plus the unaltered 750 four prestige bike.

The 125 cc MV roadster of 1976—a handsome machine (L.J. Caddell).

For a while MV had no representation in Britain, but with the 750 cc MV, Gus Kuhn Motors Ltd of South East London, became concessionaires in 1974 and began importing the 250 and 350 cc twins along with the four-cylinder 750—which was now offered at £2,200! This price included a £200 modification kit which incorporated bigger ports and hard valve springs, along with a race-type fairing.

Vincent Davey, managing director of Gus Kuhn, confirmed that interest in the twin-cylinder machines was minimal and that demand for the 750 fell away after initial orders had been met. Some 40 machines only were sold by Kuhn from 1974 until 1977 when they dropped the concession. That year MV made brave efforts to wallpaper over the cracks and, while formally they accepted their racing fate in February with an announcement confirming their retirement from the sport, they gave Britain its first chance to see the 350 cc 'Sport' twin and the 140 mph, 750 cc 'America' four when these machines were displayed at the North West Motor Cycle Show in Blackpool.

By this time an amalgamation with the already government-controlled Ducati concern had come about and—a far cry from the days when the original Count Agusta controlled every nut and bolt of the operation—MV Agusta was now in the hands of a finance group, a move inspired by the Italian Government. The fear was that MV would lose its identity through economic streamlining of manufacturing facilities, but early in 1977 an astonishing undertaking, in the circumstances, was given by the finance group with the declaration that MV machines would be produced for many years to come. World demand for MV machines was said to have reached a new high level with West Germany opening up as a valuable market, the new 'America' MV taking some of the traditional BMW market.

All this was encouraging news for Agusta Concessionaires (GB) Ltd, a newly-formed company which began importing MVs in 1977. Marketing director Peter Bate said: 'As we have now had official confirmation of MV's continued production for a minimum of 15 years and with new machines in development, we feel extremely confident'—and he began a dealer appointment programme with an initial target figure of 25 dealerships in Britain.

The optimism seemed justified. By May came the first news and pictures of a new MV engine, a four-cylinder across the frame design capable of development to any capacity from 750 to 1,200 cc. The exhaust camshaft was driven by chain, linked by an idler gear to the intake camshaft; other features included four angled cylinders and wet sump, six-gear transmission and final drive by chain. The prototype was scheduled for introduction at the Milan Show in November that year, with production beginning in 1978. Agusta Concessionaires carried the momentum to Britain later in the year by persuading MV to dig out from under dust covers in a corner of the Gallarate factory the historic 500 cc works bike which had been ridden to World Championship victories by Agostini and Read. They brought it to London for the Earls Court Motor Cycle Show in 1977, and also spotlighted the 350 Agusta 'Sport', the 750 'America' and the newer 'bigger bore' version, the 850 cc 'America' SS.

At this stage the official line was one of optimism. They were not in the mass market but, with a small but skilled workforce in Italy, the 750 S 'America', a restyled 750 MV original, and 350 models, represented MV's determined penetration of the elite motor cycle market by producing some of the finest machines available at the time. Later, the 850 cc MV was also claimed to be selling well in the UK. However, if you wanted the quality you had to pay the price, for in 1977 the 350 cc MV retailed at £1,299 (including VAT) and the 'America' was then the most expensive motor cycle on sale in Britain at £3,187. It was also, claimed the importers, the fastest with a top speed of 140 mph.

These two machines are best remembered in Britain from the final days of MV. Specifications as follows:

MV 350 cc

Engine	Twin-cylinder four stroke. Overhead valve pushrod and rocker operated. Bore and stroke 63 mm × 56.2 mm. Capacity 349 cc. Compression ratio 9.5:1. Carburation: 2 Dell'Orto VHB 24 B. Claimed power output: 40 bhp at 8,500 rpm. Wet sump lubrication.
Transmission	Primary drive by gears. Multiplate clutch in oil. Five-speed gearbox with right side change lever. Overall ratios: 1st, 11.68:1; 2nd 8.45:1; 3rd 6.47:1; 4th 5.44:1; 5th 4.98:1.
Electrical	12-volt battery and 80-watt flywheel generator. 60-watt headlamp bulb.

Brakes	Front—twin hydraulically operated discs. Rear—single hydraulic disc.
Tyres	Metzeler: front, 2.50 in × 18 in; rear, 3.50 in × 18 in.
Dimensions	Wheelbase 53$\frac{1}{2}$ in: overall length 78 in; ground clearance 6.5 in.
Fuel capacity	4$\frac{1}{4}$ gallons.

MV 750 S 'America'

Engine	Double overhead camshaft, in-line, four-cylinder. Light alloy barrels and one-piece cylinder head. Five roller main bearings; roller big ends. Gear change to camshafts from centre of crankshaft. Bore and stroke 67 mm × 56 mm. Capacity 790 cc. Compression ratio 10.2:1. Carburation: 4.26 mm choke Dell'Orto VHB. Claimed power output: 86 bhp at 8,500 rpm. Wet sump lubrication.
Transmission	Primary spur gears. Multiple clutch in oil. Five-speed gearbox. Overall ratios: 1st 11.68:1; 2nd 8.45:1; 3rd 6.47:1; 4th 5.44:1; 5th 4.98:1.

Electrical	12-volt battery and 135-watt dc generator and starter-motor combined. 60-watt headlamp bulb.
Brakes	Front—twin hydraulically operated discs. Rear—single hydraulic disc.
Tyres	Metzeler: front, 3.50 in × 18 in; rear, 4.00 in × 18 in.
Dimensions	Wheelbase 55 in, overall length 83 in, ground clearance 5.3 in.
Fuel capacity	4$\frac{1}{2}$ gallons.

For many enthusiasts the MV 750 was the most handsome of the superbikes and the most impressive two-wheeler on the market and MV Agusta were to keep the flag flying right up to the end on the domestic front. In May 1978, came reports that an impressive limited production 1,000 cc-plus MV was to be introduced into the German market. This new monster was said to have an actual capacity of 1,066 cc and a major departure was the switch to chain final drive. Top speed was put at around 145 mph and the price, in Germany, around £7,750. The factory claimed that the entire first batch were sold even before they arrived from Italy.

It was a final, magnificent gesture worthy of the dramatic nature of MV's presence on the race circuits of the world over more than 20 years, for in that same year—1978—MV Agusta were to cease all motor cycle production.

Chapter 17

The end of the road

By 1975 the glory days for MV Agusta were at an end. Driven into complacency by years of easy victories, with no urgent need to build substantially new machinery, MV had dropped far behind the Japanese opposition. The passionate dream and galvanising dedication of Domenico Agusta had disappeared with his death and while Corrado Agusta battled manfully for a time to maintain the proud tradition, a new more commercial era had arrived. MV found themselves a little out of their depth. They stuck to old fashioned principles, even when it came to essential sponsorship. For a long time they brushed aside any suggestion of financial help and even when Elf, the French petrol giant, eventually got an agreement to help with running costs—it was said to be to the tune of about £100,000—there was still a lot of hard talking to be done before MV agreed to Elf stickers going on those classic machines.

Phil Read was undecided about the new season. In Japan he test-rode works Suzukis and was known to have been in contact with Kawasaki. He was keen for a 750 cc ride to complement his grand prix outings—which he could not get with MV in 1975. Also the Italian factory made him angry when they attempted to veto his choice of race clothing, including helmet, which would have broken an important sponsorship deal he had arranged. Finally, the disputes were sorted out and he decided to stay with MV. Franco Bonera was signed to ride alongside him. Meantime, Agostini re-signed for Yamaha and so the battle between Yamaha and MV, Agostini and Read, which had kept the 500 cc World Championship electrically alive in 1974, was set to be re-activated for the new season.

Yamaha had worked hard on their machinery during the winter. So had MV. To enable Dunlop ultra-wide slicks to be used, wider rear forks were built and they also put a lot of effort into gaining more stability at the back, experimenting with a variety of rear-suspension layouts. One system incorporated a modified frame with rear suspension units inclined forward to allow more travel, while another used a cantilever layout bringing them really up-to-date. Despite the effort, there was little joy for MV in the early season Italian meetings. The cantilever frame was abandoned after disappointing tests early in the year at the Paul

Ricard circuit and at Misano Agostini shattered all opposition, including MV, by taking his Yamaha to two record-breaking victories. Phil Read's more traditional MV four had shown good promise early on and was leading the race for the first few laps. Then a misfire led to retirement when two plugs oiled up. Bonera, on the second MV, finished a reasonable second. At Modena, however, in the final showing before the opening of the grand prix season, MV Agusta were decisively beaten by Yamaha. Read complained of acute handling problems, almost dropping the bike on the second lap, and he never really recovered, finishing well behind Agostini. There were further problems for MV as Bonera crashed in practice, breaking a leg. Promising 23-year-old Italian Armando Toracca was drafted into the team as a replacement on a race-to-race basis.

MV's problems mounted at the Paul Ricard circuit for the opening round of the season, the French Grand Prix. Still troubled by handling problems, Read crashed heavily in practice damaging the little finger on his right hand, the finger that had given persistent trouble since his Imola crash two years before. The machine was badly damaged in the crash. MV's practice times were disappointing, Toracca being in fourth position behind Lansivuori (Suzuki), Agostini and Kanaya (Yamahas). Read was fifth fastest, after his Italian team mate, having been forced to switch to the cantilever-framed MV four. In the race, before a record 120,000 fans at the 3.2-mile French circuit, the MVs made an encouraging start. On top speed the Italian machines were a match for the Yamahas and Phil took up the challenge from the second row of the grid, going quickly to the front, ahead of Agostini and Toracca. However, at the end of the important first lap, Agostini led from the two MVs with Kanaya on the second Yamaha in fourth position. Then, with a shattering burst of speed, Lansivuori hurtled the Suzuki first past Toracca, then Read, then Agostini, to take up the running, racing well ahead. He looked a certain winner until gearbox trouble on the new Suzuki put him out of touch. Meanwhile, Read and Toracca could not get the MVs to handle properly and although their machines had ample speed on the straights, they lost ground seriously on the corners as the riders struggled to control them. Agostini took the Yamaha to victory, the MVs finishing third (Read) and fourth.

The MV's handling problems caused urgent concern at Gallarate. Phil Read took British frame expert Ken Sprayson to the factory early in April and at about the same time Ducati racer and tester Bruno Spaggiari spent a day with the MV team at Modena. This latter move set up a certain amount of friction between Read and the factory chiefs. Phil took Spaggiari's involvement as a reflection by the MV bosses on his ability as a rider and was happier later in the season when Luigi Ghisleri, reputedly responsible for asking Spaggiari to test the machines, moved into MV's production department and Fredmano Spairani was put in charge of racing.

In the next World Championship round, in Spain, there was no 500 cc race, but Agostini built up his confidence and did nothing to help MV's, by taking his Yamaha to a storming 350 cc victory. Austria was the scene for the next round and, at the famous Salzburgring, MV had a better day. At one point Toracca on the second MV led the other four works machines in the race but, with Agostini's Yamaha suffering an electrical fault which led to his withdrawal after appearing in comfortable command, and with Read's MV no match for the better handling Yamaha and Suzuki two-strokes, the race ended with a third and fourth for MV (Read and Toracca) behind winner Kanaya (Yamaha) and Lansivuori (Suzuki).

Read was battling hard to retain his title, but at this point was struggling. The initiative rested with Agostini as they set off for the West German Grand Prix at Hockenheim. Before 130,000 fans, Phil must have sensed that the championships were at a critical stage and he pulled out all the stops in a sensational bid to get the MV ahead of Agostini's Yamaha. The two riders battled wheel-to-wheel for most of the race and Read, riding the MV four which had been fitted with a new cylinder head and modified forks, raced to the limit, shattering the Italian's morale as he stood on the footrests in valiant attempts to control the machine. From the start Toracca had gone sensationally into the lead. Read took over on the second lap as Agostini came storming up to overtake Toracca. As Toracca retired with a dead magneto, Agostini closed on Read and the battle was on. It was one of the finest, all-action 500 cc battles for years. Lap after lap the two riders treated the crowd to a breathtaking spectacle, battling side by side, but as Read tried everything he knew to get ahead, Agostini countered successfully and his Yamaha had the extra speed

to give him the advantage. After more than 80 gruelling miles Agostini took the Yamaha across the line with less than four seconds to spare after setting a new absolute lap record for the West German circuit at 110.94 mph.

It had been a sensational race in which Phil Read diced with disaster a number of times. The closest he came to crashing was on the sweeping right hander at the end of the circuit when travelling at about 120 mph half-way through the race. On the corners Agostini, because the Yamaha handled better, was able to cut back some of the advantage Phil had gained on the more open sections because of the MV's superior speed. Read flung the MV into the corner and with the machine well cranked over, hit a bump and the exhaust pipe grounded. The back end of the machine lifted and the speeding bike slid sideways for about 60 to 70 yards. To keep control Phil had literally to stand up on the machine, clinging to the handlebars, and was lucky to stay on the road.

Although MV had yet to win a championship race, those closely-run second places by Read had been building up the points. After Hockenheim, Kanaya, surprisingly, led the World Championship table with 35 points, Read on the MV was in second place, just three points behind and two ahead of third place man Agostini, while Toracca was in a creditable fifth position with 16 points.

A good showing in Italy, before their home crowd, would be a tremendous boost for MV, but at Imola, driven on by a patriotic crowd, Agostini had an inspired ride to win and was besieged by ecstatic fans as they realised that their national hero was at the top of the championship table for the first time that season. On the MV Read never gave up and finished in second place, half a minute behind Agostini, who was in total command. Toracca finished fourth.

As Read and Toracca strove to keep MV in the championship fight, the factory had been creating its own news. Back in April there had been strong and persistent rumours that new Venezuelan wonder-boy Johnny Cecotto had been invited to test MV machines, though MV officially denied that a direct approach had been made. The reports did not please Read, who had not been too happy about Toracca's signing, even on a race-to-race basis. The factory had acted against his declared wishes then and, if so disposed, might do so again. But any thought MV might have had for signing Cecotto was not very practical. The young and talented South American was already in line for the 250 and 350 cc world titles as well as the FIM's Formula 750 cc championship, all classes in which

Battle of the 1975 giants—Phil Read on the MV, Giacomo Agostini on a Yamaha and Barry Sheene on a Suzuki, during the 500 cc race of the Dutch TT. Read and the MV finished third (Mick Woollett).

MV had no practical interest, and it was surely stretching logic to consider that he might give all this up for the sake of an MV ride in the 500 cc class. Nothing came of the approach.

Hardly had those rumours settled than there was the shock news that MV were considering the production of a *two-stroke* 500 cc grand prix racer for 1976, a move totally alien to their consistent policy over many years of outstanding grand prix success of racing four-strokes. Behind the switch in policy was said to be MV's new racing director, Fredmano Spairani, a former director of the Ducati concern.

There was also exciting news about MV's intention to put on over-the-counter sale in 1976 a batch of 50 racing engines as a development of what seemed to be a much more commercial sense by the firm following the Italian Government's 51 per cent stake in the company. However, for racing fans, the grand prix circus was the major consideration as the riders and machines moved into Holland. Gianfranco Bonera was back in the MV saddle for the first time since his pre-season crash at Modena, but it was team leader Phil Read who shot into the lead at the start. The promise soon disappeared and, as Read was unable to keep the MV in contention after early laps, the race became a battle between Agostini on the Yamaha and Barry Sheene, back in the Suzuki saddle in a grand prix for the first time since his major crash at Daytona. Sheene outwitted Agostini over the final stretch to take the race. MV, through Read, finished third.

France, Austria, West Germany, Italy, Holland . . . and MV were still without a win. The

Belgian Grand Prix was next on the calendar and if MV Agusta were ever going to win a World Championship race in 1975 then in Belgium it surely would have to be. The ultra-fast 8.76 miles Spa-Francorchamps circuit, with the long and famous Masta Straight, was ideal for the sprinting style of the MV and history was certainly on their side. The Italian factory had won the 500 cc race there every year since 1958—an astounding record of 17 successive victories at the famous circuit. Could Read maintain the tradition?

With the MV geared up for the occasion and revving to 14,800—500 over the maximum—Phil was in his element on the sweeping circuit and he gave a pulverising display to score an exciting victory for his first maximum points of the season. A crowd of 135,000 saw Phil take command as, one by one, his challengers fell away. Agostini went out on the fifth lap with a broken seal on the Yamaha's water pump. Sheene, fighting neck and neck with Read for the lead after shattering the MV rider's existing lap record with a speed of 135.75 mph, more than 2 mph faster than Read's 1974 record, stopped with engine trouble. Read's MV team mate Bonera also retired.

MV's first grand prix victory of 1975 was an enormous boost to morale. Read with only one win against Agostini's three, reckoned he could still take the title, even though he recognised that the MV was less competitive than Agostini's Yamaha. Over the past two years improvements had been made to the MV, but it was still basically the same machine, but with the Swedish round next, to be followed by the final rounds in Finland and Czechoslovakia, the MV camp was reasonably optimistic, particularly as attempts had been made to lower the weight of the machine in an effort to improve handling. The Anderstorp circuit in

Start of the 500 cc Czechoslovakian Grand Prix of 1975 with Read on the MV (1) and Agostini on the Yamaha (4) (Mick Woollett).

Phil Read climbs the winners rostrum at Brno after winning the 500 cc Czechoslovakian Grand Prix of 1975. Though MV won the race, they were to lose the title after 17 consecutive victories (Mick Woollett).

Sweden was by no means Read's favourite but, on the other hand, he had finished second there in 1974 and had even raced the MV to victory in the 500 cc event the previous year. Since then, however, a young rider named Barry Sheene had been making his mark and on the powerful Suzuki at Anderstorp in 1975 he soon took command, after Agostini and Read had led from the start. As Sheene moved further ahead and it became obvious that the MV was no match for Agostini's Yamaha on the day, Read's hopes of retaining the 500 cc title seemed to be fast disappearing. Then he had a stroke of luck which kept him on the championship trail with an outside chance. With only two laps to go, in second place ahead of Read, Agostini crashed, letting the MV through to take second position behind Sheene.

Two rounds only left and in Finland, on the 3.74-mile Imatra circuit, the MV's reliability let Read

down for the first time in the season. The race sparkled as Read, Agostini and Bonera—two MVs and a Yamaha—fought for the initiative. Until disaster struck and the MV failed with a faulty magneto, Read had looked like getting the better of the battle. After Read's departure, Bonera caused problems for Agostini, but then the second MV rider collided with Armando Toracca, out of favour with MV and now on a Suzuki, and came down dislocating a shoulder.

Only a miracle could now give MV the title they had held for so long. Read would need to win in Czechoslovakia and even then Agostini had only to finish in the first seven to top him and take the title. On the Brno circuit, Read took the MV to its second win of the season. He rode a good race, but Agostini refused to be drawn into combat and it was Sheene and Lansivuori who put pressure on the MV rider.

111

Barry was wheel-to-wheel with Phil until, after three laps, he went out with engine problems. The battle was now taken up by Lansivuori, who maintained the pressure on Read until he went out with clutch trouble near the end. Agostini, meantime, had a comparatively easy race to finish second, behind Read's MV, for the world title.

MV Agusta had finally yielded their 500 cc World Championship after a sensational 17 years, a phenomenal record. It was Yamaha's first world title. Read declared: 'I'm only lending Agostini the title. I want it back next year'. Whether he would be back on MV, however, was anyone's guess. In October, Read met Count Corrado Agusta in an effort to sort out a contract for 1976, his current arrangement with MV finishing at the end of 1975, and although he had failed to bring MV the 500 cc title by only a narrow margin, he was insisting on a more competitive machine for 1976. A further problem was Phil's declared interest in riding in the developing FIM Formula 750 cc class, including the prestigious Daytona 200 meeting. While MV had been promising a 750 cc machine for some time—and some early work had certainly been done—the project, according to informed sources at Gallarate, had still to receive the official sanction of Corrado.

The hope was that MV would enter 750 cc racing with a new engine designed by Ing Bocchi, who had joined the factory in 1974 as race engineer after being with a number of famous car firms, including Lamborghini and Ferrari. The engine, designed as a 500 cc unit, would be capable of being enlarged for 750 cc racing. MV had shown interest in a 750 as long ago as 1972, when they had attempted unsuccessfully to convert a 750 cc roadster into a racing machine. In 1975 Alberto Pagani predicted that MV would enter 750 cc racing when the class gained World Championship status. Pagani, who rode MV machines in 1973, was now working on machine development for MV. He said that to win with a 750 would then be of great prestige value, particularly as MV intended to sell new-look road machines of 750 cc capacity.

For 1976 MV had been working hard on the flat four boxer engine which they hoped would form the basis of their grand prix challenge, but growing unrest in Italy resulting in widespread strikes and industrial disruption was feared might spread to the MV plant and hold up development. Another unfortunate move was the election of a new board of directors on the public-owned parent company now controlling MV. This added further to the uncertainty about MV's racing future for the new administration was said to be less sympathetic to motor cycling needs.

Not all was calm in opposing camps either. Barry Sheene was expected to remain with Suzuki for 1976, but Agostini was anything but happy as Yamaha announced a cut-back in their racing effort. This led him into talks with would-be sponsors after deciding he might like to form his own team. Meantime, MV had been giving rider tests to a number of Italian youngsters, including Otello Buscherini, the new 500 cc junior champion Vanes Francini, and 23-year-old Edoardo Elias, which seemed to suggest some continuing interest in racing.

Everything came to a head in December and was sparked off by persistent rumours that Agostini might return to MV in 1976 in a sensational move. This was in spite of Read's offer to stay on to help MV with the development of the new flat four boxer engine, a project in which he had already been heavily involved. Early in the month Read spoke to Count Corrado Agusta and was told that no plans about MV's racing policy for 1976 could be made until the new 500 cc boxer flat four machine had been tested, in January or February. He asked Read to wait until then before completing his own plans for the new season, but Phil explained that if in the end MV decided not to race in 1976, and it seemed a distinct possibility, then it might be too late for him to negotiate an alternative contract.

After bringing MV two 500 cc World Championships, Phil Read made his decision, quit the company and decided to look around for other rides in 1976. Within a couple of weeks, just a few days before Christmas, Giacomo Agostini was invited to Casina Costa to be told that MV were pulling out of grand prix racing, for 1976 at least, but would like him to race their machines in this team on a private basis. The idea was for the Italian World Champion to race 350 cc and 500 cc MVs in the World Championships in 1976 under the Team Agostini banner. MV would provide technical help, but Agostini would not be under contract, leaving him free to race other makes of machine in the 750 cc series.

It seemed like an ideal arrangement. It solved MV's cash and organisational problems in the short term and Agostini was drawn to the idea because of his past, phenomenally successful, association with the factory. Team manager Arturo Magni expected the new four-stroke engine to be bench tested in February and to be available for Agostini as soon as it was race ready, though in early rounds he would probably have to make do with four-cylinder machines of the type raced by Phil Read during '75.

Arturo Magni, who spent almost a lifetime with the Italian factory, with Agostini during MV's early glory years (Mick Woollett).

One key figure who perhaps more than anyone hoped that MV Agusta would retain a racing interest was their team manager, the man behind MV's remarkable catalogue of racing successes, Arturo Magni. In 1975 he celebrated 25 years with the famous Italian factory. At race circuits all over Europe Magni had provided the drive and experienced guidance for MV racing, being witness to their greatest successes. He was born near Arcore, home of Gilera, and a shared interest in aero-modelling with Ferruccio Gilera, son of the then boss of the famous Italian factory, let him into Gilera's racing department in 1947 after Arturo had been made redundant after the Second World War when the aircraft factory in which he worked closed. In 1950 he moved to MV Agusta at the start of a life-long career with the Gallarate concern. A whole vista of motor cycle racing history had passed before his eyes as he saw riders like Les Graham, Gary Hocking, Mike Hailwood, Giacomo Agostini and Phil Read, together with a great many others, in their turn race to immortality on the scarlet and silver machines which were his responsibility. In his 25 years with MV one of his greatest moments was when the three-cylinder 350 cc machine won the West German Grand Prix on its debut race in 1965. His saddest was during that same year, when a machine failure in the Japanese Grand Prix let Honda through to lift the 350 cc crown by just six championship points.

Chapter 18

A spirited finale

For 1976 the old firm were back in business and the new partnership looked promising. With backing from Api, the Italian petrol company, and Marlboro cigarettes, the 33-year-old reigning 500 cc World Champion, Giacomo Agostini, was confident. He could see no reason why he should not retain the 500 cc on the MV, win the 750 cc championship on the Yamaha, and recapture the 350 cc title for MV. A new frame was promised for the 350 cc machine and a revised unit incorporating new cylinders and head was said to have reached 75 bhp at 17,000 rpm on the bench.

It took less than six weeks for the new alliance to turn sour. After both his 350 and 500 cc MV fours had shown themselves uncompetitive at the early season meeting at Misano, Agostini was ready to quit. The 500 handled so badly that the World Champion was in danger of being lapped by race leader Marco Luccinelli on a Suzuki four. He retired rather than suffer the indignity. On the 350

Popular among the Italian crowds. Giacomo Agostini signs autographs for his fans at Imola (Mick Woollett).

machine he started well but was soon overtaken and was down to seventh when he retired. Agostini demanded an audience with Corrado Agusta and the meeting seemed to calm him down. It has to be realised that he was desperate to keep at least one world title and had nailed his flag to MV's mast. In the end he agreed to race the MVs in the opening round in France in April, where MV had a large group of mechanics in support. The new 350, revving to 16,000 rpm, topped the leaderboard in practice and justified its promise in the race, for a time. From pole position, Agostini hurtled into the lead in a race which brought the magnificent sight and sound of the 350 cc MV back to grand prix racing for the first time since 1974. But halfway round the first lap, the MV was caught by Walter Villa on a new Harley-Davidson. Villa moved ahead, with Agostini second and Johnny Cecotto third. After three laps the MV swept once more into the lead with such authority that Agostini looked set for a dramatic win. Then, just as dramatically, he was out of the race with ignition failure.

The 500 cc class was expected to be more competitive than ever in 1976. After a lot of investment Suzuki were now coming through as a major force with Barry Sheene leading the challenge. Phil Read was back on a Life International Suzuki, Johnny Cecotto had a remarkably fast Yamaha and other strong contenders were Lucchinelli and Lansivuori, also on Suzukis and Victor Palomo on a Yamaha. Even against such strong opposition the MV at first looked as though it might be a threat, but it just did not have the speed of the two-strokes and in the end Agostini did well to climb through the field to finish in fifth position behind Sheene, Cecotto, Lucchinelli and Lansivuori.

MV's hopes in the 500 cc class suffered a further setback in Austria, in the second round. Agostini was never able to get the out-paced 500 up among the leaders and finished in sixth place. The 350 cc MV was a much better proposition. For a time it looked to be very quick as Agostini, from an unimpressive start, climbed up to sixth place. As Cecotto pulled away at the head of the race, the MV stood an excellent chance of taking second place as Agostini forced his way through and on the fifth lap had only the young Venezuelan ahead of him. Two

The MV 350 GT 'Sport' of 1976, a twin-cylinder sports machine and with a top speed in excess of 100 mph, one of the fastest 350 cc bikes available (L.J. Cadell).

more laps remained before the MV limped home into the pits with a badly slipping clutch.

An incensed Agostini could tolerate the out-dated 500 MV no longer. 'Until MV get more speed I have no chance of winning', he said, and announced that he would be switching to Suzuki in the 500 cc class for the remainder of the season. He agreed to continue racing the 350 cc MV, if the Italian factory wanted to carry on.

It was just one more problem for the trouble-torn Italian company. Although the new flat four boxer engine was now almost ready for testing, opinion inside the firm was to split, one faction taking the view that the flat four with two front facing pistons and two to the rear would be the answer to get MV back into 500 cc competition. The other, led by team manager Arturo Magni, favoured a flat engine with all four cylinders facing forwards. Even more basic was Count Corrado's problem: could MV *afford* to invest in the development necessary to take on the Japanese, and what of the whole future

of MV motor cycles, now that the Italian Government was substantially running the show?

For the time being, MV decided to withdraw from the 500 cc championship, but took up Agostini's offer to carry on in the 350 cc series. In Italy and Yugoslavia, the 350 cc MV proved fast but unreliable. Fourth fastest in practice in Italy, Agostini shot into the lead from the start of the race and headed the pack before pulling out, complaining that his machine was undergeared. Second fastest in practice in Yugoslavia, the MV was again off to a magnificent start, chasing the Finnish rider, Pentti Korhonen, and Tom Herron. Agostini moved to the front at the end of the opening lap and stayed there for another 14 laps, before he pulled into the pits with a holed piston.

It was sad to see the once most successful and exciting racing factory eclipsed so conclusively, but of the World Championship rounds remaining in 1976, Holland and West Germany were to stand out as memorials to the glorious traditions of MV

A close-up of the instrument panel on the MV 350 'Sport' (L.J. Cadell).

Agusta. Earlier, the Italian company had shown its resilience by approaching Marco Lucchinelli, the 22-year-old Italian then lying second to Barry Sheene in the 500 cc World Championship table, with an offer of MV 500 cc rides, but he turned them down. This disappointment was soon forgotten as Agostini took the 350 cc MV to a sensational victory in Holland. It was the first 350 cc win for MV since the Finnish Grand Prix back in 1973.

Everything clicked neatly into place on the day and Agostini ran a superb race. Victor Palomo led from the line with the MV in third place, but Agostini was at the front by the end of the first lap and looked a winner from then on. After three laps he was 11 seconds clear, increasing the gap to 21 seconds after 11 laps. Racing magnificently through the 'S' bend at the back of the pits with his chest flat on the tank and without easing back the throttle, Agostini proved himself once more an outstanding rider and he completed the 16 laps of the newly revised 4.8-mile Assen circuit 24 seconds ahead of second placed Patrick Pons. The MV also set the fastest lap at 94.28 mph.

It was a text-book swansong for the 350 cc MV,

for to add to MV's troubles, their most effective machine was now outlawed by the FIM's new noise regulations due to come into force the following month. To bring the 350 cc machine down to the new permitted noise levels would mean a 15 per cent power reduction and there seemed to be no effective way that silencers could be fitted to the machines. Moreover, their new flat four was hardly likely to fare better under the new regulations. With no 350 cc races on the programme for the next two grands prix, in Belgium and Sweden, MV perhaps had time to come up with an answer, but in the meantime the Belgian round closed the door firmly on a racing era. Every year since 1956 the 500 cc Belgian Grand Prix had been won by MV Agusta—a magnificent total of 20 consecutive victories, but in 1976 the run ended as John Williams took his Suzuki across the line first, with MV not even represented in the race.

There was no joy for MV in Finland, nor Czechoslovakia, for although the 350 cc machine *did* appear, in Finland Agostini retired after five laps with a burnt-out coil. He had blown up the good engine in practice and had done well on the hastily rebuilt machine to reach second place behind Walter Villa before being forced out. In Czechoslovakia, the MV did not even make the front row of the grid and at the end of the second lap was in the pits with a broken valve and holed piston.

MV had not yielded easily to providence and in July Agostini tested a 500 cc MV four with a new frame which, if promising, could be available for racing towards the end of the season. At the Nürburgring, for the final round in the series—the West German Grand Prix, Agostini rode both his Suzuki and the new MV in practice. In the dry the MV would still be uncompetitive, considered Agostini, even without Barry Sheene racing, the Suzuki rider already having made sure of the 500 cc world title. But in the wet the legendary combination of Agostini and the famous four-stroke MV could prove decisive.

It was dark and overcast as Agostini, his decision made, brought the MV to the line for the start of the race. It was to be an inspired ride. So good was Agostini's performance on the first lap that from a standing start he lapped the 14.19-mile circuit in 9 mins 13.8 secs to set a new class record, faster even than Jarno Saarinen's previous absolute circuit best. He was even quicker the second time round at 9 mins 1.1 secs and was now 9 secs clear of the chasing Lansivuori. Before it started to rain Agostini's 14 second lead after three laps had been cut to 12 after four, but in the wet the MV steadily gained ground and completed the seven laps with a comfortable 52 seconds margin over second placed rider Lucchinelli.

It was an emotional moment as Agostini climbed the winner's rostrum, for although the outstanding Italian rider was to continue racing for a little longer, it was effectively the end for MV Agusta. The last racing appearances of MV in Britain took place towards the end of the year with Phil Read riding the 500 at Cadwell Park and Giacomo Agostini on the magnificent 350 at Brands Hatch— worthy gestures to the fans who had given so much respect and support to MV during their happier days.

Chapter 19

The last years

The fight to keep MV Agusta alive as a motor cycle company went on for many months and may not be entirely over, even now. First defences were set up within the company itself. The business had been founded on motor cycles and while helicopters brought in the money, the factory, for virtually its entire life, had related closely to motor cycle racing. Such a heritage could not be allowed to disappear overnight. For a long time Count Corrado Agusta looked for ways of keeping things going. In the unique situation which had existed when Domenico was at the helm, racing had altogether claimed too much time and resources to make economic sense for MV. By the time Corrado took over, the Italian

era in motor cycles was approaching its end, beaten into the ground by its own complacency and the Japanese.

The efforts MV Agusta made to establish export markets for their motor cycles were too feeble and, perhaps, came too late. Their market research seemed questionable and against the stream of new, exciting and updated models which continued to flow from the Japanese giants, their new machines took a long time to see the light of day and were expensive, even allowing for their obvious quality and superior, up-market image.

Instability and unrest in Italy itself did not help MV's problems and the situation came to a head

Phil Read riding the 500 cc MV at Cadwell Park (B.R. Nicholls).

A close-up of the 350 four-cylinder MV of 1977 (Mick Woollett).

when the Italian Government secured a controlling interest in the firm. Perhaps now the motor cycle organisation would be re-established on a sounder base, but the truth was that the government was attracted to MV Agusta because of their flourishing helicopter business and the gestures they made towards keeping the motor cycle business going could not in the long term be substantiated.

Racing, on which the factory had built its name, was the first to suffer. Against the power of the commercial Japanese factories, MV seemed incapable of getting back on competitive terms and even towards the end of 1976 it was obvious that unless they could come up with something positive, there was little point in continuing in grand prix racing.

For a while they picked at the problem, tinkering with modified parts and localised improvements, though it's true that the 1976 350 cc machine was faster than earlier versions, but unfortunately it was not reliable. Sadly, the racing flat four boxer engine, where they had directed their big effort and in which they had sunk their hopes for the future, proved unsuccessful during bench tests and was not competitive enough to be introduced as an immediate replacement for the four-cylinder engines used in 1976.

In Britain, local news of MV had seemed more optimistic. Peter Bate, of Agusta Concessionaires (GB) Ltd, announced that he would be importing the sleek looking 350 cc 'Sport' and the 750 S 'America' road machines and he took over Mallory Park for a dealer presentation as a springboard to the setting up of a national dealer network. Reaction was good, Peter Bate confirmed recently, and of the 100 dealers present some 30 signed a letter of intent to become dealers. But rumours of MV's difficulties back in Italy broke the very next week and from then on Bate's enterprise was doomed.

When they took control the Italian Government confirmed the future of MV Agusta motor cycles and statements are on record which talk about new investment, new machines and future development. Later, when the hard, commercial decisions had to be made, the confidence in MV Agusta as a maker and seller of motor cycles at profitable levels, was simply not forthcoming. Sales of new models were, generally, disappointing. The 750 'America' had been built to capture a slice of the North

American market but sales and distribution problems took their toll and by the time things were sorted out, it was too late anyway. It was obvious that public money could be better used on the helicopter side of the business, which was profitable, expanding and carried far brighter prospects.

Peter Bate says the middle of the 1970s was the time when things began to go wrong. 'That is when the motor cycle side of things started to be run by helicopter men', he said recently. Before moving in on MV, the Italian Government had taken over Ducati, another Italian motor cycle company, and they invested large sums of money in both concerns. It seemed a natural consequence when, towards the end of 1976, it was announced that the two firms were to be amalgamated. A directive from the government put Ducati in charge of all future MV

motor cycle production and, more significantly, decreed no more direct finance for racing. It was a grim picture as a run-down of motor cycle production at the historic Gallarate factory began. MV Agusta, as we had known it, was at an end.

One hope remained. Count Corrado Agusta was a rich man and was known to have been enthusiastic about bike racing in his earlier days. Would he be prepared to finance the race organisation out of his personal fortune, helped perhaps by major sponsorship? Sadly, this kind of swashbuckling initiative belonged to a past age and those classic MV Agusta race machines just disappeared from the circuits. It may have been different had MV kept more in step with developments over the years. But it was clear that too much money would be at too much risk to keep idealism alive.

From Britain, operating on behalf of a third

Agostini taking the famous MV 500 to its last grand prix win in Germany in 1977 (Mick Woollett).

party, Peter Bate tried desperately to salvage something from the wreckage. His instructions were to buy the manufacturing rights and finance the production of MV's road-going bikes, but negotiations with the government representatives and official bodies proved impossible. Said Peter Bate recently: 'The money was available. We even chartered a plane, organised currency exchange formalities and had a member of the British Consulate smoothing the way for us, but with a cheque literally in our hands ready to hand over, the officials representing MV's interests said they just couldn't take a decision'.

It all became incredibly complicated, time was running out and eventually efforts were abandoned. In October 1978 Agusta Concessionaires (GB) Ltd was closed down and Peter Bate returned to the motor trade, where he had been employed before taking an interest in MV. Over in Italy, the once famous racing department was closed, race team manager Arturo Magni moved away to set up his own business specialising in MV tuning kits at Samarate, close to Milan, and the historic premises at Verghera which had developed some of the finest race machines in the world, were taken over completely for helicopters.

End of story? Who knows? For a time the sport forgot about MV Agusta and that superb sound of those roaring four-strokes as Suzuki and Yamaha blazed the grand prix glory trail, but then MV Agusta flashed once more into the news as former works rider Franco Bonera and two go-ahead Italian enthusiasts, Claudio and Gianfranco Castiglioni, took steps to revive the MV name. It seemed at first like an impossible dream, but the Cagiva motor cycle manufacturing company, through the Castiglioni brothers' enterprise, had grown out of the former Italian Aermacchi/HD concern, investing heavily in its take-over and development. Talks with MV opened, almost broke down, but Cagiva pursued the objective of acquiring the rights to use the MV name. With the deal would go the famous race machines and at the end of February, 1979, Luigi Giacometti, sales director of Cagiva, was sufficiently confident to announce that, while no agreement had yet been concluded, it was hoped to race the 350 cc MVs during 1979. Gianfranco Bonera and Marco Lucchinelli were to be approached as possible riders.

The idea at first would be to race the machines in Italian events only, but a move back into grand prix racing would surely be a strong possibility once the original machines had been made competitive. Many experts felt that the engine of the 350 MV would still be highly competitive, though it would need an entirely new frame. But with the 350 cc class due to be phased out of the World Championships in 1980, any future hopes for MV in grand prix racing would have to rest with the 500 cc machine. Whether such an ambitious move, if it did see the light of day, could be a success is open to speculation. Since the days when MV and Agostini ruled from Spain to Yugoslavia, Sweden to Italy, modern technology has taken motor cycle racing into a new age and it would surely require quite enormous investment to make room at the top once more for MV Agusta.

The decline of MV was sad to watch. The one-man crusade started by Domenico from the small village of Verghera all those years ago is still remembered with great affection and the gap which appeared when the renowned four-strokes finally left the racing arena has, for many purists, never been completely filled by the screaming two-strokes of Yamaha and Suzuki, however fast and exciting these machines undoubtedly are. For when Phil Read rode the aged MV at Cadwell Park in a final flourish in September 1976 his home was reportedly flooded with telegrams and telephone calls from enthusiasts thanking him for riding the MV once more.

Appendix

MV Agusta—World Championship record

In the 25 years, 1952 to 1976, MV Agusta won:
* 38 individual World Championships
* 37 manufacturers World Championships
* 270 World Championship races.

Individual World Championships

1952	125 cc	C. Sandford
1955	125 cc	C. Ubbiali
1956	125 cc	C. Ubbiali
	250 cc	C. Ubbiali
	500 cc	J. Surtees
1958	125 cc	C. Ubbiali
	250 cc	T. Provini
	350 cc	J. Surtees
	500 cc	J. Surtees
1959	125 cc	C. Ubbiali
	250 cc	C. Ubbiali
	350 cc	J. Surtees
	500 cc	J. Surtees
1960	125 cc	C. Ubbiali
	250 cc	C. Ubbiali
	350 cc	J. Surtees
	500 cc	J. Surtees
1961	350 cc	G. Hocking
	500 cc	G. Hocking
1962	500 cc	M. Hailwood
1963	500 cc	M. Hailwood
1964	500cc	M. Hailwood
1965	500 cc	M. Hailwood
1966	500 cc	G. Agostini
1967	500 cc	G. Agostini
1968	350 cc	G. Agostini
	500 cc	G. Agostini
1969	350 cc	G. Agostini
	500 cc	G. Agostini
1970	350 cc	G. Agostini
	500 cc	G. Agostini
1971	350 cc	G. Agostini
	500 cc	G. Agostini
1972	350 cc	G. Agostini
	500 cc	G. Agostini
1973	350 cc	G. Agostini
	500 cc	P. W. Read
1974	500 cc	P. W. Read

Manufacturers World Championships

1952	125 cc
1953	125 cc
1955	125 cc, 250 cc
1956	125 cc, 250 cc, 500 cc
1958	125 cc, 250 cc, 350 cc, 500 cc
1959	125 cc, 250 cc, 350 cc, 500 cc
1960	125 cc, 250 cc, 350 cc, 500 cc
1961	350 cc, 500 cc
1962	500 cc
1963	500 cc
1964	500 cc
1965	500 cc
1967	500 cc
1968	350 cc, 500 cc
1969	350 cc, 500 cc
1970	350 cc, 500 cc
1971	350 cc, 500 cc
1972	350 cc, 500 cc
1973	500 cc

World Championship Races

Argentine

1963	500 cc	M. Hailwood

Austria

1971	350 cc	G. Agostini
	500 cc	G. Agostini
1972	350 cc	G. Agostini
	500 cc	G. Agostini

Belgium

1956	125 cc	C. Ubbiali
	(also 2nd, Libanori)	
	250 cc	C. Ubbiali
	(also 2nd, Taveri)	
	350 cc	J. Surtees
	500 cc	J. Surtees
1957	250 cc	J. Hartle
1958	350 cc	J. Surtees
	(also 2nd, Hartle)	
	500 cc	J. Surtees
	(also 3rd, Hartle)	
1959	125 cc	C. Ubbiali
	(also 2nd, Provini)	
	500 cc	J. Surtees
1960	250 cc	C. Ubbiali
	(also 2nd, Hocking and 3rd, Taveri)	
	500 cc	J. Surtees
	(also 2nd, Venturi)	
1961	500 cc	G. Hocking

1962	500 cc	M. Hailwood
1963	500 cc	M. Hailwood
1964	500 cc	M. Hailwood
1965	500 cc	M. Hailwood
	(also 2nd, Agostini)	
1966	500 cc	G. Agostini
1967	500 cc	G. Agostini
1968	500 cc	G. Agostini
1969	500 cc	G. Agostini
1970	500 cc	G. Agostini
1971	500 cc	G. Agostini
1972	500 cc	G. Agostini
	(also 2nd, Pagani)	
1973	500 cc	G. Agostini
	(also 2nd, Read)	
1974	500 cc	P. W. Read
1975	500 cc	P. W. Read

Czechoslovakia

1968	350 cc	G. Agostini
	500 cc	G. Agostini
1969	350 cc	G. Agostini
	500 cc	G. Agostini
1970	350 cc	G. Agostini
1972	500 cc	G. Agostini
1973	500 cc	G. Agostini
	(also 2nd, Read)	
1974	500 cc	P. W. Read
	(also 2nd, Bonera)	
1975	500 cc	P. W. Read

East Germany

1961	350 cc	G. Hocking
	500 cc	G. Hocking
1962	500 cc	M. Hailwood
1963	350 cc	M. Hailwood
	500 cc	M. Hailwood
1964	500 cc	M. Hailwood
1965	500 cc	M. Hailwood
	(also 2nd, Agostini)	
1966	350 cc	G. Agostini
1967	500 cc	G. Agostini
1968	350 cc	G. Agostini
	500 cc	G. Agostini
1969	350 cc	G. Agostini
	500 cc	G. Agostini
1970	350 cc	G. Agostini
	500 cc	G. Agostini
1971	350 cc	G. Agostini
	500 cc	G. Agostini
1972	350 cc	P. W. Read
	500 cc	G. Agostini

Finland

1963	350 cc	M. Hailwood
	500 cc	M. Hailwood

1965	350 cc	G. Agostini
	500 cc	G. Agostini
1966	500 cc	G. Agostini
1967	500 cc	G. Agostini
1968	500 cc	G. Agostini
1969	350 cc	G. Agostini
	500 cc	G. Agostini
1970	350 cc	G. Agostini
	500 cc	G. Agostini
1971	350 cc	G. Agostini
	500 cc	G. Agostini
1972	350 cc	G. Agostini
	500 cc	G. Agostini
	(also 2nd, Pagani)	
1973	350 cc	G. Agostini
	500 cc	G. Agostini
	(also 2nd, Read)	
1974	500 cc	P. W. Read
	(also 2nd, Bonera)	

France

1955	125 cc	C. Ubbiali
	(also 2nd, Taveri)	
1959	350 cc	J. Surtees
	(also 3rd, Hartle)	
	500 cc	J. Surtees
	(also 2nd, Venturi)	
1960	350 cc	G. Hocking
	500 cc	J. Surtees
	(also 2nd, Venturi)	
1961	500 cc	G. Hocking
1969	500 cc	G. Agostini
1970	500 cc	G. Agostini
1972	500 cc	G. Agostini
1973	350 cc	G. Agostini
	(also 2nd, Read)	
1974	500 cc	P. W. Read

Germany

1953	125 cc	C. Ubbiali
1955	125 cc	C. Ubbiali
	(also 2nd, Taveri and 3rd, Venturi)	
1956	250 cc	C. Ubbiali
	(also 2nd, Taveri and 3rd, Venturi)	
1957	125 cc	C. Ubbiali
	(also 3rd, Colombo)	
	250 cc	C. Ubbiali
	(also 2nd, Colombo)	
1958	125 cc	C. Ubbiali
	(also 2nd, Provini)	
	250 cc	T. Provini
	500 cc	J. Surtees
	(also 2nd, Hartle)	

1959	125 cc	C. Ubbiali	**1969**	350 cc	G. Agostini
	(also 2nd, Provini)			500 cc	G. Agostini
	250 cc	C. Ubbiali	**1970**	350 cc	G. Agostini
	350 cc	J. Surtees		500 cc	G. Agostini
	(also 3rd, Brambilla)		**1971**	350 cc	G. Agostini
1959	500 cc	J. Surtees		500 cc	G. Agostini
	(also 2nd, Venturi)		**1972**	350 cc	G. Agostini
1960	250 cc	G. Hocking		500 cc	G. Agostini
	(also 2nd, Ubbiali)			(also 2nd, Pagani)	
	500 cc	J. Surtees	**1973**	350 cc	G. Agostini
	(also 2nd, Venturi and			(also 2nd, Read)	
	3rd, Mendogni)			500 cc	P. W. Read
			1976	500 cc	G. Agostini

Holland

1952	125 cc	C. Sandford
1955	125 cc	C. Ubbiali
	(also 2nd, Venturi)	
	250 cc	L. Taveri
	(also 2nd, Lomas and	
	3rd, Masetti)	
1956	125 cc	C. Ubbiali
	(also 2nd, Taveri)	
	250 cc	C. Ubbiali
	(also 2nd, Taveri)	
	500 cc	J. Surtees
1957	500 cc	J. Surtees
1958	125 cc	C. Ubbiali
	(also 3rd, Provini)	
	250 cc	T. Provini
	(also 2nd, Ubbiali)	
	350 cc	J. Surtees
	(also 2nd, Hartle)	
	500 cc	J. Surtees
	(also 2nd, Hartle)	
1959	125 cc	C. Ubbiali
	250 cc	T. Provini
	(also 2nd, Ubbiali)	
	500 cc	J. Surtees
	(also 3rd, Venturi)	
1960	125 cc	C. Ubbiali
	(also 2nd, Hocking)	
	250 cc	C. Ubbiali
	(also 2nd, Hocking and	
	3rd, Taveri)	
	350 cc	J. Surtees
	(also 2nd, Hocking)	
	500 cc	R. Venturi
	(also 3rd, Mendogni)	
1961	350 cc	G. Hocking
	500 cc	G. Hocking
1962	500 cc	M. Hailwood
1964	500 cc	M. Hailwood
1965	500 cc	M. Hailwood
	(also 2nd, Agostini)	
1968	350 cc	G. Agostini
	500 cc	G. Agostini

Isle of Man

1952	125 cc	C. Sandford
1953	125 cc	L. Graham
	(also 3rd, Sandford)	
1955	125 cc	C. Ubbiali
	(also 2nd, Taveri)	
	250 cc	B. Lomas
1956	125 cc	C. Ubbiali
	250 cc	C. Ubbiali
	(also 2nd, Colombo)	
	500 cc	J. Surtees
1958	125 cc	C. Ubbiali
	250 cc	T. Provini
	(also 2nd, Ubbiali)	
	350 cc	J. Surtees
	500 cc	J. Surtees
1959	125 cc	T. Provini
	250 cc	T. Provini
	(also 2nd, Ubbiali and	
	3rd, Chadwick)	
	350 cc	J. Surtees
	(also 2nd, Hartle)	
	500 cc	J. Surtees
1960	125 cc	C. Ubbiali
	(also 2nd, Hocking and	
	3rd, Taveri)	
	250 cc	G. Hocking
	(also 2nd, Ubbiali)	
	350 cc	J. Hartle
	(also 2nd, Surtees)	
	500 cc	J. Surtees
	(also 2nd, Hartle)	
1962	350 cc	M. Hailwood
	(also 2nd, Hocking)	
	500 cc	G. Hocking
1963	500 cc	M. Hailwood
1964	500 cc	M. Hailwood
1965	500 cc	M. Hailwood
1966	350 cc	G. Agostini
1968	350 cc	G. Agostini
	500 cc	G. Agostini

1969	350 cc	G. Agostini
	500 cc	G. Agostini
1970	350 cc	G. Agostini
	500 cc	G. Agostini
1971	500 cc	G. Agostini
1972	350 cc	G. Agostini
	500 cc	G. Agostini
	(also 2nd, Pagani)	

Italy

1952	500 cc	L. Graham
1954	125 cc	G. Sala
	(also 3rd, Ubbiali)	
1955	125 cc	C. Ubbiali
	(also 2nd, Venturi and	
	3rd, Copeta)	
	250 cc	C. Ubbiali
	500 cc	U. Masetti
1956	125 cc	C. Ubbiali
	250 cc	C. Ubbiali
	(also 3rd, Venturi)	
1957	125 cc	C. Ubbiali
	(also 3rd, Taveri)	
	350 cc	J. Surtees
	(also 2nd, Hartle)	
1958	500 cc	J. Surtees
	(also 2nd, Venturi and	
	3rd, Masetti)	
1959	250 cc	C. Ubbiali
	350 cc	J. Surtees
	(also 2nd, Venturi)	
	500 cc	J. Surtees
	(also 2nd, Venturi)	
1960	125 cc	C. Ubbiali
	(also 2nd, Spaggiari)	
	250 cc	C. Ubbiali
	350 cc	G. Hocking
	500 cc	J. Surtees
	(also 2nd, Mendogni)	
1961	350 cc	G. Hocking
	(also 2nd, Hailwood)	
	500 cc	M. Hailwood
1962	500 cc	M. Hailwood
	(also 2nd, Venturi)	
1963	500 cc	M. Hailwood
1964	500 cc	M. Hailwood
1965	350 cc	G. Agostini
	500 cc	M. Hailwood
	(also 2nd, Agostini)	
1966	350 cc	G. Agostini
	500 cc	G. Agostini
1967	500 cc	G. Agostini
1968	350 cc	G. Agostini
	500 cc	G. Agostini

1970	350 cc	G. Agostini
	(also 2nd, Bergamonti)	
	500 cc	G. Agostini
	(also 2nd, Bergamonti)	
1971	500 cc	A. Pagani
1972	350 cc	G. Agostini
	500 cc	G. Agostini
	(also 2nd, Pagani)	
1973	350 cc	G. Agostini
1974	500 cc	G. Bonera
	(also 3rd, Read)	

Japan

| 1965 | 350 cc | M. Hailwood |

Northern Ireland

1952	125 cc	C. Sandford
	(also 2nd, Lomas and 3rd, Salt)	
1956	125 cc	C. Ubbiali
	(also 3rd, Webster)	
	250 cc	L. Taveri
1957	125 cc	L. Taveri
	(also 3rd, Venturi)	
1958	125 cc	C. Ubbiali
	250 cc	T. Provini
	350 cc	J. Surtees
	(also 2nd, Hartle)	
	500 cc	J. Surtees
	(also 3rd, Hartle)	
1959	350 cc	J. Surtees
	500 cc	J. Surtees
	(also 2nd, Venturi)	
1960	125 cc	C. Ubbiali
	(also 2nd, Hocking)	
	250 cc	C. Ubbiali
	350 cc	J. Surtees
	(also 2nd, Hartle)	
1961	350 cc	G. Hocking
	500 cc	G. Hocking
1962	500 cc	M. Hailwood
1967	350 cc	G. Agostini
1968	350 cc	G. Agostini
	500 cc	G. Agostini
1969	350 cc	G. Agostini
	500 cc	G. Agostini
1970	350 cc	G. Agostini
	500 cc	G. Agostini

Spain

1952	500 cc	L. Graham
1953	125 cc	A. Copeta
	(also 2nd, Sandford)	
1954	500 cc	D. Dale
	(also 3rd, Pagani)	
1955	125 cc	L. Taveri
	(also 3rd, Ubbiali)	

1961	250 cc	G. Hocking
1968	500 cc	G. Agostini
1969	350 cc	G. Agostini
	500 cc	G. Agostini
1970	350 cc	A. Bergamonti
	500 cc	A. Bergamonti
1973	500 cc	P.H. Read

Sweden

1959	125 cc	T. Provini
	(also 2nd, Ubbiali)	
1960	350 cc	J. Surtees
	(also 2nd, Hartle)	
1961	500 cc	G. Hocking
	(also 2nd, Hailwood)	
1971	350 cc	G. Agostini
	500 cc	G. Agostini
1972	350 cc	G. Agostini
	(also 2nd, Read)	
	500 cc	G. Agostini
1973	500 cc	P.H. Read
	(also 2nd, Agostini)	

United States

| 1964 | 500 cc | M. Hailwood |
| 1965 | 500 cc | M. Hailwood |

West Germany

1961	500 cc	G. Hocking
1964	500 cc	M. Hailwood
1965	350 cc	G. Agostini
	(also 2nd, Hailwood)	
	500 cc	M. Hailwood
	(also 2nd, Agostini)	
1967	500 cc	G. Agostini
1968	350 cc	G. Agostini
	500 cc	G. Agostini
1969	350 cc	G. Agostini
	500 cc	G. Agostini
1970	350 cc	G. Agostini
	500 cc	G. Agostini
1971	350 cc	G. Agostini
	500 cc	G. Agostini
1972	500 cc	G. Agostini
	(also 2nd, Pagani)	
1973	500 cc	P.H. Read
1976	500 cc	G. Agostini

Yugoslavia

1970	350 cc	G. Agostini
	500 cc	G. Agostini
1972	500 cc	A. Pagani

Index